Rational Emotive Behavior Therapy
Second Edition

Theories of Psychotherapy Series

Theories of Psychotherapy Series

Matt Englar-Carlson, Series Editor

Rational Emotive Behavior Therapy

Second Edition

Albert Ellis and Debbie Joffe Ellis

AMERICAN PSYCHOLOGICAL ASSOCIATION
Washington, DC

Published by
American Psychological Association
750 First Street, NE
Washington, DC 20002
www.apa.org

APA Order Department
P.O. Box 92984
Washington, DC 20090-2984
Phone: (800) 374-2721; Direct: (202) 336-5510
Fax: (202) 336-5502; TDD/TTY: (202) 336-6123
Online: http://www.apa.org/pubs/books
E-mail: order@apa.org

In the U.K., Europe, Africa, and the Middle East, copies may be ordered from
Eurospan Group
c/o Turpin Distribution
Pegasus Drive
Stratton Business Park
Biggleswade, Bedfordshire
SG18 8TQ United Kingdom

Phone: +44 (0) 1767 604972
Fax: +44 (0) 1767 601640
Online: https://www.eurospanbookstore.com/apa
E-mail: eurospan@turpin-distribution.com

Typeset in Minion by Circle Graphics, Inc., Reisterstown, MD

Printer: Sheridan Books, Chelsea, MI
Cover Designer: Beth Schlenoff Design, Bethesda, MD
Cover Art: *Lily Rising*, 2005, oil and mixed media on panel in craquelure frame, by Betsy Bauer

Library of Congress Cataloging-in-Publication Data
Names: Ellis, Albert, 1913-2007, author. | Joffe-Ellis, Debbie, 1956- author.
Title: Rational emotive behavior therapy / Albert Ellis and Debbie Joffe Ellis.
Description: Second [edition]. | Washington, DC : American Psychological
  Association, [2019] | Series: Theories of psychotherapy series | Includes
  bibliographical references and index.
Identifiers: LCCN 2018048696 (print) | LCCN 2018049043 (ebook) |
  ISBN 9781433830938 (eBook) | ISBN 1433830930 (eBook) | ISBN 9781433830327
  (pbk.) | ISBN 1433830329 (pbk.)
Subjects: LCSH: Rational emotive behavior therapy.
Classification: LCC RC489.R3 (ebook) | LCC RC489.R3 E4647 2019 (print) |
  DDC 616.89/14—dc23
LC record available at https://lccn.loc.gov/2018048696

British Library Cataloguing-in-Publication Data
A CIP record is available from the British Library.

Printed in the United States of America

http://dx.doi.org/10.1037/0000134-000
10 9 8 7 6 5 4 3 2 1

We dedicate this book to students, therapists, teachers, and all those who create unnecessary emotional suffering in their lives. May you benefit from applying rational emotive behavior therapy in your lives and sharing it—to help you and others experience great joy in life, despite and including its challenges.

Contents

Series Preface

S ome might argue that in the contemporary clinical practice of psychotherapy, the focus on evidence-based intervention and effective outcome have overshadowed theory in importance. Maybe. But, at the same time it is clear that psychotherapists adopt and practice according to one theory or another because their experience, and decades of good evidence, suggests that having a sound theory of psychotherapy leads to greater therapeutic success. Theory is fundamental in guiding psychotherapists in understanding *why* people behave, think, and feel in certain ways, and it provides guidance to then contemplate *what* a client can do to instigate meaningful change. Still, the role of theory in the helping process can be hard to explain. This narrative about solving problems helps convey the importance of theory:

> Aesop tells the fable of the sun and wind having a contest to decide who was the most powerful. From above the earth, they spotted a man walking down the street, and the wind said that he bet he could get his coat off. The sun agreed to the contest. The wind blew, and the man held on tightly to his coat. The more the wind blew, the tighter he held. The sun said it was his turn. He put all of his energy into creating warm sunshine, and soon the man took off his coat.

What does a competition between the sun and the wind to remove a man's coat have to do with theories of psychotherapy? This deceptively simple story highlights the importance of theory as the precursor to any effective intervention—and hence to a favorable outcome. Without a guiding theory, a psychotherapist might treat the symptom without understanding the role of the individual. Or we might create power conflicts with our clients and not understand that, at times, indirect means of helping (sunshine) are often as effective—if not more so—than direct ones (wind). In the absence of theory, we might lose track of the treatment rationale and instead get caught up in, for example, social correctness and not wanting to do something that looks too simple.

What exactly *is* theory? The *APA Dictionary of Psychology* defines *theory* as "a principle or body of interrelated principles that purports to explain or predict a number of interrelated phenomena" (2nd ed., VandenBos, 2015, p. 1081). In psychotherapy, a theory is a set of principles used to explain human thought and behavior, including what causes people to change. In practice, a theory creates the goals of therapy and specifies how to pursue them. Haley (1997) noted that a theory of psychotherapy ought to be simple enough for the average psychotherapist to understand but comprehensive enough to account for a wide range of eventualities. Furthermore, a theory guides action toward successful outcomes while generating hope in both the therapist and client that recovery is possible.

Theory is the compass that allows psychotherapists to navigate the vast territory of clinical practice. In the same ways that navigational tools have been modified to adapt to advances in thinking and ever-expanding territories to explore, theories of psychotherapy have evolved over time. The different schools of theories are commonly referred to as *waves*, the first wave being psychodynamic theories (i.e., Adlerian, psychoanalytic); the second wave, learning theories (i.e., behavioral, cognitive behavioral); the third wave, humanistic theories (i.e., person-centered, gestalt, existential); the fourth wave, feminist and multicultural theories; and the fifth wave, postmodern and constructivist theories (i.e., narrative, solution-focused). In many ways, these waves represent how psychotherapy has adapted and responded to changes in psychology, society, and epistemology as well as to changes in the nature of psychotherapy itself. The wide variety of theories is also testament to the different ways in which the same human behavior can be conceptualized depending on the view one espouses (Frew & Spiegler, 2012). Our theories of psychotherapy are also challenged to expand beyond the primarily Western worldview endemic in most theories and the practice of psychotherapy itself. That requires theories and psychotherapists to become more inclusive of the full range of human diversity to reflect and understanding of human behavior that accounts for a client's context, identity, and intersectionality (American Psychological Association, 2017). To that end, psychotherapy and the theories that guide it are dynamic and responsive to the changing world around us.

It is with these two concepts in mind—the central importance of theory and the natural evolution of theoretical thinking—that the American Psychological Association (APA) Theories of Psychotherapy Series was developed. This series was created by my father (Jon Carlson) and myself. Although educated in different eras, we both had a love of theory and often spent time discussing the range of complex ideas that drive each model. Even though my father identified strongly as an Adlerian and I was parented and raised from this perspective, my father espoused an appreciation for other theories and theorists—and that is something I picked up from him. As university faculty members teaching courses on the theories of psychotherapy, we wanted to create learning materials that not only highlighted the essence of the major theories for professionals and professionals-in-training but also updated readers on the current status of the models. Often in books on theory, the biography of the original theorist overshadows the evolution of the model. In contrast, our intent is to highlight the contemporary uses of the theories as well as their history and context.

As this project began, we faced two immediate decisions: which theories to address and who best to present them. We looked at graduate-level theories of psychotherapy courses to see which theories are being taught, and we explored popular scholarly books, articles, and conferences to determine which theories draw the most interest. We then developed a dream list of authors from among the best minds in contemporary theoretical practice. Each author in the series is one of the leading proponents of that approach as well as a knowledgeable practitioner. We asked each author to review the core constructs of the theory, bring the theory into the modern sphere of clinical practice by looking at it through a context of evidence-based practice, and clearly illustrate how the theory looks in application.

There are 24 titles planned for the series, and many titles are now in their second edition. Each title can stand alone or be grouped together with other titles to create materials for a course in psychotherapy theories. This option allows instructors to create a course featuring the approaches they believe are the most salient today. APA Books has also developed a DVD for each of the approaches that demonstrates the theory in practice with a real client. Many of the DVDs show psychotherapy over six sessions with the same client. For a complete list of available DVD programs, visit the APA website (http://www.apa.org/pubs/videos). Most programs are also available in streaming format.

Albert Ellis was one of a kind. Recognized as the first to move the practice of psychotherapy into the cognitive realm, his contribution to the field of psychotherapy is immeasurable. If there was a Mount Rushmore of psychotherapy, Al's would be one of the four faces. It was an honor that the first edition was among the final publications in Al's distinguished career that included over 750 scholarly articles and books. As a young graduate student, I was fortunate to attend one of Al's "Five-Dollar Friday Night Workshops" in New York City. Though I was raised Adlerian, rational emotive therapy (as it was known at the time) was the first approach to psychotherapy that truly clicked with my own understanding of the field. My father (Jon Carlson) was friends with both Al and Debbie, and with the passing of my father and Al, Debbie and I have continued to maintain our own friendship. For the first and second edition, I appreciate Debbie Joffe Ellis's skill and craft in keeping Al's words and thoughts alive. In many ways, our intersecting relationships and this monograph have provided personal and professional satisfaction.

Al created rational emotive behavior therapy (REBT) through experience and through trial and error. He discovered that applying traditional analytic methods did not produce the results that contemporary society desired. REBT became an effective brief therapeutic approach and the forerunner to other cognitive approaches to psychotherapy. The theoretical model provides a holistic understanding of human behavior that shows how thoughts, feelings, and cognitions interact. As you read this book, note how this model allows the practitioner to effectively sift through the client's narrative to discover areas of therapeutic intervention.

—Matt Englar-Carlson

How to Use This Book With APA Psychotherapy Videos

E ach book in the Theories of Psychotherapy Series is specifically paired with a DVD that demonstrates the theory applied in actual therapy with a real client. Many DVDs feature the author of the book as the guest therapist, allowing students to see an eminent scholar and practitioner putting the theory they write about into action.

The DVDs have a number of features that make them excellent tools for learning more about theoretical concepts:

- Many DVDs contain six full sessions of psychotherapy over time, giving viewers a chance to see how clients respond to the application of the theory over the course of several sessions.
- Each DVD has a brief introductory discussion recapping the basic features of the theory behind the approach demonstrated. This allows viewers to review the key aspects of the approach about which they have just read.
- DVDs feature actual clients in unedited psychotherapy sessions. This provides a unique opportunity to get a sense of the look and feel of real psychotherapy, something that written case examples and transcripts sometimes cannot convey.
- There is a therapist commentary track that viewers may choose to play during the psychotherapy sessions. This track gives unique insight into why therapists do what they do in a session. Further it provides an in vivo opportunity to see how the therapist uses the model to conceptualize the client.

The books and DVDs together make a powerful teaching tool for showing how theoretical principles affect practice. In the case of this book, the DVD *Rational Emotive Behavior Therapy,* which features the author as the guest expert, provides a vivid example of how this approach looks in practice.

Acknowledgments

The first edition of *Rational Emotive Behavior Therapy* was one of the final books that my husband, Dr. Albert Ellis, and I worked on before his passing in New York City on July 24, 2007. I continue to profoundly love and honor the life, spirit, and brilliance of my husband as I continue the work of rational emotive behavior therapy (REBT), and I remain grateful for and in awe of his massive contributions to our field and beyond.

My heartfelt thanks to Tim Runion, with great appreciation for his usual typographical excellence and his outstanding generosity.

I also remember with deep gratitude the late Jon Carlson, who, along with his son Matt, invited Al and me to write the first edition of this book. Jon's contributions to psychology and counseling were immense, and his work done in front of and behind the scenes continues to help countless numbers of people. Jon was a dear and encouraging friend to me and was deeply supportive of my mission to teach, share, practice, and expand people's knowledge and awareness of REBT.

Thank you, Jon.

Rational Emotive Behavior Therapy
Second Edition

Introduction

Almost all humans have the goals of staying alive and being happy. Too many people are unaware that it is not outer events or circumstances that will create happiness; rather, it is our perception of events and of ourselves that will create, or uncreate, positive emotions. People who are aware that they control their emotional and behavioral destinies have a far greater chance of experiencing more joy, less misery, and a healthy stability, even when coping with hardships. How? They choose to think in rational, realistic, and life-enhancing ways. In so doing, appropriate and healthy emotions and actions result.

From its start, rational emotive behavior therapy (REBT), the pioneering cognitive behavior therapy (CBT), has taught that when people want to survive and be happy, they then have several desires: to perform important tasks well, to relate successfully to others, and to do what it takes to help them reach their goals. When they strongly desire to achieve

http://dx.doi.org/10.1037/0000134-001
Rational Emotive Behavior Therapy, Second Edition, by A. Ellis and D. Joffe Ellis

or avoid something, their wishes and wants frequently (and unhealthily) escalate into needs or necessities. They also frequently and falsely convince themselves that "when I perform well, I am a good person; if I perform badly, I am bad." Just as they harmfully globally rate themselves as "good" or "bad," they rate others as "great" or "damnable." Similarly, they globally rate the world or life-as-a-whole as "good" or "bad."

Seen in the context of REBT, by thinking, feeling, and acting in these irrational and inaccurate ways (and by refusing to accept others and life unconditionally), people can often unhealthily defeat their goals and purposes. They also needlessly create problems such as the unhealthy negative emotions of severe anxiety, depression, and rage. By refusing to accept themselves unconditionally, people needlessly, again, create guilt, shame, and self-loathing, in addition to any or all of the previously noted unhealthy emotions (A. Ellis, 2005b).

Constructivism holds that people have considerable power to construct self-helping thoughts, feelings, and actions, as well as to construct self-defeating behaviors. It is fortunate that despite this tendency to act destructively, people also have the tendency to act constructively if they so choose. Similar to Kelly's (1955) theory of personal constructs, REBT hypothesizes that people have choice, to some degree, in how they conduct their lives and, with some degree of effort, can change themselves considerably, despite any biological or societal limitations.

Because of their constructivism, people can motivate and force themselves to change. Having highly developed language systems, they can think, think about their thinking, and think about thinking about their thinking. Even though their thinking, feeling, and actions may seem to be separate or disparate, they influence and interact with one another. When people think, they also feel and act. When they feel, they also think and act. When they act, they also think and feel. By recognizing that they are thinking, feeling, or behaving in destructive ways, people have the ability to push themselves to think, feel, and act in healthy and rational ways.

Consequently, REBT teaches many kinds of thinking, feeling, and behavioral techniques to identify, investigate, and change dysfunctional behaviors. It is holistic in approach. It is multimodal in its methods. It holds that steady work and practice is usually required to change destructive tendencies and acts and to maintain desired changes.

REBT vigorously encourages insight, realistic perspective, reasoning, and logic but holds that these rational elements alone—without strong emotion, motivation, and action—are not enough for lasting change.

REBT is highly educational. Direct didactic teaching of its theories and practices often works, so it uses dialogue, arguing, and disputing of irrational beliefs with clients. It also uses other educational approaches, such as articles, books, lectures, workshops, CDs, and DVDs. It recognizes that indirect teaching methods can work well with many people and therefore uses Socratic dialogue, stories, fables, plays, poems, parables, and other forms of communication. It strongly acknowledges that each person is an individual who may find that particular modalities of learning work best for him or her.

REBT is the founding cognitive, multimodal, and integrative therapy approach. Albert Ellis originated it in the 1950s, and other cognitive approaches followed.[1] From its start, the approach included philosophical as well as experiential, emotional, and behavioral techniques. As its creator and founder, Al was ostracized and criticized by most of the psychological, psychiatric, and social professions in the early years of REBT. He and his approach were referred to as superficial, simplistic, and worse by some members of the psychoanalytic community; others reacted to his writings and lectures with anger, intellectual dissent, and arrogance. This is not surprising: Psychoanalysis was the dominant therapeutic approach of the day, and he was challenging most of its major assertions and tenets!

The cognitive approach and REBT (or main aspects of it) appear now to be used by a strong majority of practitioners in the helping professions. Beginning in the 1960s, studies showed that people who hold irrational

---

[1]Note for readers: Albert Ellis passed away in 2007, during the process of writing the first edition of this book. He continued to present on REBT until months before his death in July 2007. Although hospitalized and in a rehabilitation care facility for his final 14 months of life, he taught psychology and counseling students and others who would come for that purpose to the care home and to the hospital. He also continued to give interviews to journalists and professors and attend to writing and other matters, as much as his health and strength would allow. In this book, the authorial "I" refers to the second author, Debbie Joffe Ellis. I continue to present and write on REBT in the United States and abroad.

beliefs are significantly more disturbed than when they do not hold them, and the more strongly they hold them, the more disturbed they tend to be (A. Ellis & Whiteley, 1979). Al and his colleagues started doing outcome studies; then Aaron Beck, Donald Meichenbaum, and others began to do them; and now there are thousands of studies on the effectiveness of CBT. The studies tend to show that when people change their rigid, irrational beliefs to flexible nondogmatic preferences, they become less disturbed.

One thing that distinguishes REBT from most other CBTs is its strong philosophical emphasis. It is humanistic and existential. Unlike other cognitive approaches, it strongly and vigorously emphasizes the importance of unconditional acceptance. It aims to help people achieve the three basic REBT philosophies of unconditional self-acceptance, unconditional other-acceptance, and unconditional life-acceptance. To do this, it uses cognitive, emotional, and behavioral methods, which are all described in this book. It also reminds people of the benefit and power of gratitude (D. J. Ellis, 2015)

REBT also differs from theories of the other CBTs in its assumption that the basic philosophies or core irrational beliefs that many people usually follow to make themselves disturbed largely involve their adopting and creating absolutistic musts. Although most of the popular CBTs include these musts, they do not emphasize—as REBT does—how basic and underlying they are and how they lead to most other profound disturbances, such as awfulizing, low frustration tolerance, and self-denigration. REBT most vigorously urges people to change their core irrational self-defeating philosophies and champions precision in the disputing process.

Although the REBT therapist is taught to practice unconditional other-acceptance with clients, he or she is not to encourage or foster dependence of the client on him or her. A major goal of REBT is to encourage people to be largely self-sufficient and empowered to choose healthy ways of thinking, feeling, acting, and being—and to accept themselves unconditionally even if they do not choose these healthy ways—without needing acceptance or approval from others, including their almighty therapists!

Al believed, and I still believe, that the principles of REBT should be taught in the school system, so that children can learn how to avoid disturbing themselves and how to overcome disturbance when it occurs, so that they grow into adults who think, act, and feel in healthy ways, suffer minimal misery, and experience great and substantial happiness throughout their lives.

This book gives the reader a substantial introduction to the theory and practice of REBT. This second edition of the book includes updated references and describes major emphases given to certain of the REBT aspects in recent years. It can be used in conjunction with the DVD *Rational Emotive Behavior Therapy*, part of the *Systems of Psychotherapy Video Series*, in which a clinical demonstration is given and questions are answered.[2]

I believe that REBT, with precise focus on the aspects most relevant for the here and now, has a potency and power that expedites healthy change and healing. Since the passing of Albert Ellis, it appears that large numbers of former REBT practitioners and teachers are merging REBT with CBT. As a result, some of REBT's essential elements can be neglected or underemphasized. I hope that increased research will be done that continues to show, as past studies have done, the strength and effectiveness of REBT. The principles of REBT are timeless and can benefit individuals of any culture and race; they were applicable during past times in history and are highly relevant in the present. During certain periods it can be helpful to focus more strongly than ever on particular principles: In the 21st century, so far, when mass and academic literature report that higher stress is being experienced by many, greater attention and application of REBT's encouragement to practice greater mindfulness, tolerance, unconditional acceptance, and gratitude can reduce such stress significantly. Read it, enjoy it, apply it—and keep on doing it. Although nothing in life is absolutely certain, it is highly probable that therapists, clients, students, family, and friends will all benefit greatly.

Try it and see!

---

[2]For more information, visit http://www.apa.org/pubs/videos/4310919.aspx.

2

History

In this chapter, I discuss the origins of rational emotive behavior therapy (REBT), its development, and its more recent history. Much more detail on the early days of the development is given in *All Out!: An Autobiography* (A. Ellis, 2010).

ORIGINS

Although it could be said that Albert Ellis developed REBT between 1953 and 1955 after he largely abandoned the liberal psychoanalysis he had been practicing for the previous 10 years, seeds of the theory were evident throughout times in his childhood, teens, and early adult years.

As a child, Al was often unwell and hospitalized, and his parents, who were busy—his mother with his two siblings, his father with his work and other activities—did not visit him as often as many of the parents of

http://dx.doi.org/10.1037/0000134-002
Rational Emotive Behavior Therapy, Second Edition, by A. Ellis and D. Joffe Ellis

other young patients visited their children. To lessen his sadness about this neglect, he would stop himself from dwelling on thoughts of this miserable state of affairs. He would instead busy himself by reading books, imagining and inventing grand schemes or lovely scenarios in his head, or conversing with nurses and others who were around. This was good use of the cognitive distraction method!

During his school years, Al did well in his studies and got exceptionally high grades. He was given the nickname "Encyclopedia" because it was said that he knew everything. He read practically every book that he could get his hands on, which included books by ancient and modern philosophers and psychologists. Writers he had read by age 16 included Socrates, Epicurus, Epictetus, Marcus Aurelius, Seneca, Confucius, Lao Tzu, Gautama Buddha, Emerson, Dewey, Santayana, Russell, Wittgenstein, Spinoza, Kant, Hume, Thoreau, Freud, Watson, and Adler—to name only a few.

It can be said that his main influences, profoundly so, were philosophers, psychologists, essayists, novelists, dramatists, poets, and other writers. He was not a gullible believer of what he read. He thought about what he read, critically ripped up what he didn't agree with, and experimentally used aspects of what he agreed with on himself. Years later, he would use with clients what he had learned from successful application on himself.

In 1932, at age 19, he was appointed the leader of a radical youth group, which required him to speak in public. He decided he'd better work on overcoming his terror of public speaking. He used his philosophical teachings to convince himself that nothing terrible would happen if he spoke publicly and that even if he felt uncomfortable or performed poorly during the process, it wouldn't kill him. In other words, he was convincing himself of two main philosophies that he later incorporated into REBT: *unconditional self-acceptance* (i.e., unconditionally accepting oneself with one's flaws and failings, just because one exists, whether or not one performs well and gains approval from others) and *high frustration tolerance* (i.e., accepting and tolerating that which one does not want, like, or prefer). Reading about the in vivo desensitization work of John B. Watson (1919), the first behaviorist, and his assistant, Mary Cover Jones, was further encouragement to him to do what he was afraid of to overcome the fear.

And it worked! Not only was he over his fear within months of pushing himself to speak in public, he found that he enjoyed it and had a talent for it.

Then, in 1933, a month or so before his 20th birthday, he decided to use the same approach to overcome his shyness and terror of talking to women. Risking failure and rejection, he spoke to 100 women during the month of August during college summer vacation. Out of the 100 women, he made only one date—and she didn't show up! Nonetheless, he found empirically that nothing terrible happened, and he successfully overcame his fear and became good at conversing with women. He discovered the great value of cognition, philosophy, reasoning, and self-persuasion in changing one's dysfunctional feelings and actions.

He made the understanding of cognitive processes one of the main elements of the therapy he practiced with clients from 1943 to 1947 before using psychoanalytic therapy, and after he practiced psychoanalysis and found it to be just about the least efficient form of therapy ever invented, he returned to active–directive therapy in 1952 and strongly and most vigorously emphasized cognition.

His original training as a psychotherapist had been in the field of marriage, family, and sex counseling, where therapy sessions largely consisted of giving specific information to clients about effective communicating, about sex issues and what to do about sexual problems they were experiencing, about child rearing, and so on. Although the outcome of therapy in these cases was often successful, it was clear to him that if people were to be most effective at living harmoniously with others, they'd better first learn how to live peacefully with themselves. He then did a course of intensive psychoanalytic training, albeit with reservations about Freud's theory of personality. He underwent orthodox psychoanalysis with a respected analyst of the Horney group and proceeded to use this approach with his clients, increasingly feeling skepticism about its efficiency and efficacy. Even though many of his clients would feel better after sessions, they were rarely getting better in the sense of steadily experiencing less of the unhealthy emotions, such as anxiety, depression, or rage, nor did they know how they could prevent themselves from getting such disturbances. He began employing less of the drawn-out psychoanalytic approach and became increasingly active–directive, although still analytically oriented.

From 1952 to early 1955, he was one of the most active–directive psychoanalytically oriented psychotherapists in the field—and with good results.

His clients were experiencing better and more lasting results in a shorter length of time with the active–directive approach. It was becoming more and more clear to him that insight about problems was not enough to change or cure them—action that combated that which largely created the problems was required. He would vigorously encourage clients to do what they were afraid of (e.g., risk rejection) to see concretely that such things were not so fearsome. Many responded well to his urgings, but some remained resistant. They would stick with their habitual, irrational ways of thinking about themselves and others and continue to feel anxiety, hostility, and other destructive emotions. He continued to work on putting his psychological and philosophical knowledge together. He saw that people learned ideas of right and wrong and about what they should or shouldn't do from parents and others and mass societal communication—and also that they were able, because of their facility with language and thinking ability, to create their own limiting self-talk. They could create fears in their own minds that had no basis in reality. They could convince themselves—without questioning—that the irrational ideas of others were facts. If they were taught that it was terrible to be rejected, they kept telling themselves that rejection is awful. People would reindoctrinate themselves with the nonsense they were indoctrinated with from their early years.

As he continued to work away from psychoanalytically oriented therapy to REBT, it was more and more apparent to him that his clients were not merely indoctrinated with irrational mistaken ideas of worthlessness when they were very young, but that they then continued to believe these ideas during adulthood. They actively kept reindoctrinating themselves with the original nonsense, making it an integral part of their philosophy of life. Continuing to believe unrealistic harmful ideas, as well as the tendency to define things as "terrible" when they were in fact simply inconvenient or unpleasant, was a large part of the reason that clients remained stuck in their neuroses. Seeing clearly that neurotic behavior is not merely externally conditioned or indoctrinated in childhood but that it is also internally reindoctrinated by the individual to himself or herself, he radically shifted his work. Instead of simply showing them how they'd originally become disturbed and what they could do to undo the upset, he also now focused on what they could *un-say* and *un-think* to help themselves most effectively.

He would show clients that their disturbances came largely from their believing fallacies were facts, essentially from telling themselves—and believing—a chain of false sentences. He would help clients identify and recognize their demands—the musts and shoulds of their beliefs—that were creating many of their disturbances. More and more of his clients who understood the power of their negative ideas changed these ideas—and, as a result, were less disturbed and acted differently (in goal-enhancing ways) with others. Remarkable changes occurred within relatively short periods, and by the beginning of 1955 the basic theory, principles, and practice of REBT were fairly well formulated (A. Ellis, 1994).

Al titled his first major article on REBT "Rational Psychotherapy" (1958) and deliberately emphasized the *rational* to show that it was very different from most of the existing therapies, many of which he thought were antirational. They included little on cognitive aspects, and in his work he was emphasizing thinking as well as feeling and behaving. It was a paper ahead of its time and in some ways it still is.

Al presented it at the annual convention of the American Psychological Association (APA) in Chicago on August 31, 1956 (A. Ellis, 1956), and had already given briefer versions at psychological meetings in 1955. He had written articles on the subject that were published in 1957 (A. Ellis, 1957b, 1958), but because of publication delay, this article was not published in the *Journal of General Psychology* until early in 1958.

Along with Bob Harper, his friend, colleague, and coauthor of one of his first books, *A Guide to Rational Living* (A. Ellis & Harper, 1961), Al changed the name to rational emotive therapy in 1961. They thought people would realize that it was cognitive, emotive, and behavioral, but people often got stuck on the word *rational.*

For many years after that, another good friend and colleague, Ray Corsini, advised Al to change it to rational emotive *behavior* therapy, but because rational emotive therapy was well known from his books, journal articles, and workshops, he neglected to do so until 1993, when he finally decided Ray was right. Al wrote an article for *The Behavior Therapist* that year showing that what he was doing was REBT, and that has been its name ever since (A. Ellis, 1993).

REBT is not static, and since those early years, it has been expanded and refined, with increasing research backing its premises. Al wrote more than 85 books and more than 2,000 articles. In a survey of APA's clinical and counseling psychologists, published in 1982 (Smith, 1982), Al was rated the second most influential psychotherapist (behind Carl Rogers, but ahead of Sigmund Freud). In the study by Heesacker, Heppner, and Rogers (1982), Al was found to be the most cited contributor of works published since 1957 in three major counseling journals over a 27-year period, and a study of Canadian clinical psychologists showed that he was their most influential psychotherapist, followed by Carl Rogers and Aaron Beck (Warner, 1991).

CONTEMPORARY APPROACH
AND EVOLUTION TO THE PRESENT

As noted earlier, Al originated REBT in January 1955. It was thereafter presented at APA annual conventions from August 1956 onward and also to a large reading public, particularly through his books *How to Live With a Neurotic* (1957a) and *Reason and Emotion in Psychotherapy* (1962). Aaron T. "Tim" Beck was well aware of Al's work when he claimed to originate cognitive therapy and cognitive behavior therapy (CBT) in 1963. He hinted at the crucial role of thinking and depression in his first major article (A. T. Beck, 1963). Some of the differences between his work and Al's are mainly stylistic. As Al wrote to Tim in 1979 (A. Ellis, 2010), they both directly taught people the ABCs of their disturbances (discussed in detail in the next chapter); however, whereas REBT therapists vigorously, actively, and directively dispute clients' irrational beliefs, Beck's cognitive therapists do so more indirectly and slowly. In 2003, Al (A. Ellis, 2003c) and Tim Beck and Christine Padesky (Padesky & Beck, 2003) wrote about similarities between REBT and CBT and agreed that REBT stresses philosophy along with psychotherapy, with strong emphasis on unconditional self-acceptance, unconditional other-acceptance, and unconditional life-acceptance (A. Ellis, 2005a).

I have already mentioned some of the precursors to REBT: the philosophers and writers whose books Al read and contemplated in his childhood and teen years. Writings by general semanticist Alfred Korzybski (1933) were influential, as were contemporary philosophers, including Bertrand Russell (1950). Paul Dubois (1907), who used persuasive forms of psychotherapy; Alexander Herzberg (1945), who was one of the inventors of homework assignments; and Hippolyte Bernheim (1947) and Émile Coué (1923), who used and wrote about hypnosis and persuasive active–directive approaches were, in their ways, precursors (D. J. Ellis, 2010). Al was originally trained in the Karen Horney method of psychoanalysis, and her idea about the "tyranny of the shoulds" is frequently referred to in REBT. Alfred Adler, a main REBT precursor from the psychotherapy field, said that "a person's behavior springs from their ideas," and REBT also overlaps with additional Adlerian premises, including those about social interest (Adler, 1964).

Some of the systems that have emerged into the field of psychology, such as Hayes's (Hayes, Strosahl, & Wilson, 1999) acceptance and commitment therapy, are similar in many respects to REBT but use terminology that seems to make them significantly different. To my mind, White's (White & Epston, 1990) narrative therapy includes some of REBT's basic principles without giving due credit. Glasser's (1998) choice therapy has much that is similar to REBT, but Glasser does give credit to REBT for this. Both credible and cultish "awareness" groups have incorporated REBT techniques and philosophies without giving credit—for example, Wayne Dyer (1977) was trained in and practiced REBT before writing his popular book *Your Erroneous Zones*, which presents, in my view, almost pure REBT but gives it no credit. Keyes (1972) does much the same in his book, *Handbook to Higher Consciousness*, which is largely a rewriting of A *Guide to Rational Living*, Al's book with Bob Harper (A. Ellis & Harper, 1997).

Many other writers have copied REBT theories and practices and presented them entirely as their own. Others, intentionally or not, have used central REBT tenets but credited them to other CBT authors. Originators of certain spiritual or self-development groups, such as Werner Erhard, also have used REBT principles and have given no credit. It is a pity that this goes on, but as REBT says, it's not *awful*.

Because of its effectiveness, I believe that REBT will continue steadily and solidly into the future. I will continue to urge clients to change their core irrational self-defeating philosophies. I hope that many empirical studies will be done and that additions or modifications will be made if any aspects are found to be empirically lacking. If REBT is to be changed in any way, I would hope this be done only on the basis of many hard-headed, rigorous empirical studies. I hope that more time and money will go into researching it and other cognitive–emotive–behavioral therapies: Research and more research is the concrete means for maintaining and refining its therapeutic hypotheses.

Later in his life, Al spoke about and wrote more about REBT and Buddhism and their similarities, and he and I had given workshops on this topic. He also endorsed much of Tibetan Buddhism in his later years, but he remained skeptical of a few of its mystical aspects and of some aspects of Zen Buddhism. Nonetheless, Buddhism's main principles significantly overlap with REBT philosophies. His emphasis in REBT on thinking, feeling, and action was probably influenced by his reading of Buddhist teachings when he was young—both approaches actively and directively use all three of the healthy functioning processes: cognition, emotion, and behavior. Both recommend developing keen awareness—mindfulness—and describe the importance of perception—that is, of perceiving "reality" to assess it and make helpful changes when appropriate.

Both recognize that thinking can contain many exaggerations and illusions and recommend removing these distortions. Both encourage the use of reasoning and the examination and disputation of unhelpful irrational thoughts. Both agree that, in addition to external problems, attitudes and views about these problems also create suffering—and sometimes more suffering than the external events themselves. Both include rational spirituality in being purposive and humanistic, rather than self-centered or selfish. Both actively teach unconditional acceptance in nonextreme ways, encouraging compassion for others and oneself. Both are practical and show how to live effectively in one's society. Both favor being skeptical and open-minded about adopting their own principles, encouraging people to check them against scientific methods and theories.

Although unconditional acceptance has always been a core part of the REBT philosophy, Al emphasized it more in his later years. His book *The Myth of Self-Esteem* (A. Ellis, 2005b) focuses on it. This greater specific emphasis may have been due to his applying REBT teachings to the times, which include the increased terrorist threat of the 21st century that springs largely from the absence of unconditional other-acceptance and the resultant fanatical hatred.

The increased emphasis on unconditional acceptance may also have resulted from the active application of it in his own life. Sadly, near the end of his life, directors of the institute Al founded in 1959 acted in ways that he believed were against the REBT philosophy. Without his knowledge, the mission statement was changed. In 2005, Al was dismissed from all duties at the institute and was ousted from the board, of which he had been president. In January 2006, the State Supreme Court in Manhattan ruled that the board was wrong in ousting him at a meeting from which he was excluded. The judge's decision reinstated him to the board, and he called the institute's position regarding Al "disingenuous," citing case law saying that such a "dismissal, accomplished without notice of any kind or the right of confrontation, is offensive and contrary to our fundamental process of democratic and legal procedure, fair play and the spirit of the law," (Carey, 2006). The unfair treatment even included stopping him from teaching in the institute building starting in 2005. (Al and I rented space in the building next door and continued teaching despite the imposed restrictions.) Sadly, by the end of his life, Al no longer considered the institute that bore his name to represent him or REBT principles, nor did he believe that it was any longer fulfilling his goals for the direction he wanted REBT to take. However, throughout the ordeals of the situation, he always maintained unconditional acceptance.

Not long before Al died, he wrote the following for the first edition of this book:

> When I finally kick the bucket, I entrust my wife and coauthor of this book, Debbie Joffe Ellis, to ably continue my work. As will large numbers of fine REBT-trained therapists, who stick to its principles and don't water it down, who follow and teach it, and who do their best to practice unconditional self-acceptance, unconditional other-acceptance, and unconditional life-acceptance with their clients, themselves, and other practitioners. As REBT increases and continues to be validated by research, it is likely that more people will see that although it is not the only kind of therapy that works, in all probability, it is a better kind of therapy for more people, more of the time. (A. Ellis & D. J. Ellis, 2011)

Al died on July 24, 2007, disaffiliated from the institute bearing his name, deeply sad that it was not moving in the direction he wanted, and with pending lawsuits against certain of the directors there incomplete. More about that chapter in our lives is described in the transcript of a presentation Al gave at the end of 2005, which appears in his autobiography *All Out!* (A. Ellis, 2010, pp. 548–557).

Today, I continue to teach, write, update some former writings by Al, and give presentations in New York City where I am based, in other cities throughout the United States, and in various countries around the world. I present to academics, psychologists, counselors, and other health care practitioners, including medical doctors. I also present to groups from other fields and to members of the general public. The Department of Clinical and Counseling Psychology at Columbia University Teachers College offers a full-semester course of REBT, which I teach (in the very same building in which Al studied and gained his master's and PhD). Sadly, his premonition that REBT might be watered down or merged with more general CBT is proving true in the work of many who had studied and worked with him, though others (including myself) are not doing so. It is important to mention that REBT is a very flexible and multimodal approach, and, as is mentioned in this book, certain REBT aspects, which are not so much focused on in other cognitive approaches, are emphasized more in current times than they may have been 60 years ago. My desire to not dilute REBT's offerings through merging and omission does not in any way diminish the acknowledgment by Al and me of the excellence of other approaches such as CBT. I simply want to underscore the benefit of maintaining REBT's uniqueness, boldness, and at times idiosyncratic contributions when teaching and applying it. I do not intend to discourage practitioners from choosing or adding other modalities to their work. I simply desire to provide solid and precise education in the REBT approach and to encourage practitioners to have the opportunity to substantially learn all elements of REBT as designed by its brilliant creator and which has been and continues subsequently, by this author and others, to be made relevant, undiluted, for the here and now.

3

Theory

In this chapter, I discuss the theory behind rational emotive behavior therapy (REBT). The goals of REBT are simple, the primary one being to help as many people as possible to suffer less and to enjoy life more.[1]

REBT also aims to provide people with the knowledge and tools to make this main goal possible in clear and easy-to-understand language. It can be more than simply an effective evidence-based approach—it can also be a way of life for those people who apply it as such. It strives to train effective teachers and practitioners of the approach to share REBT with their clients and students and to encourage members of the public to read recommended books and attend presentations and workshops on the subject. It encourages people to act on what they learn. Insight alone is generally not enough to create beneficial and lasting change. Ongoing

---

[1]The key concepts of REBT are discussed at length in A. Ellis (1962, 2001b, 2005b) and A. Ellis and Harper (1961, 1975, 1997). The development of certain core REBT concepts from Al's personal experiences are discussed at length in A. Ellis (2010).

http://dx.doi.org/10.1037/0000134-003
Rational Emotive Behavior Therapy, Second Edition, by A. Ellis and D. Joffe Ellis

work and practice are required. To reach these goals in therapy, a practitioner uses the theory behind the approach. I provide an introduction to this theory here.

WHAT WE TELL OURSELVES: RATIONAL AND IRRATIONAL THINKING

The basic principles of REBT include the following:

- It is not what happens that creates our emotions and actions, but what we tell ourselves about what happens. In other words, people do not upset themselves merely because of unfortunate *adversities* (A) that occur in their lives, but also with *beliefs, feelings, and behaviors* (B) that they add to these adversities. Therefore, A plus B equals their disturbed (or nondisturbed) *consequences* (C). They partly construct their disturbed (and nondisturbed) feelings by reacting (B) to undesirable As. They create and control their emotional and behavioral destiny by the way they think.

- REBT takes a holistic view of the interconnectedness and interrelatedness among our thoughts, feelings, and behaviors—that is, people's contributions at B to C consist of thoughts, feelings, and behaviors, all of which collectively lead to their healthy and unhealthy consequences. When As are viewed as "bad," people have rational or sensible beliefs–feelings–behaviors at B, such as, "I don't like As and wish they didn't exist. But they do exist and I can cope with them." They then feel what REBT calls *healthy reactions*, such as sorrow, disappointment, and frustration. These healthy reactions enable them to cope with adversities (As). When people view their adversities as "terrible" and "awful" and think they "can't stand them," they have irrational beliefs–feelings–behaviors and instead react at C with depressed, angry, and anxious reactions. They feel disturbed and cope poorly with adversities (As).

    For example, let's say that at A someone verbally abused you or falsely accused you of some heinous action, and at C you felt unhealthily enraged. It would not have been the abuse or accusations at A that caused your C, but your beliefs at B. In all likelihood you would have thought something such as, "He *should* not have spoken to me like that, *damnable* creature that he is. People *should* treat me nicely all the time, and with respect, and *never* falsely accuse me. It is *awful* he did that, and I just *can't stand him.*"

If at B, you had told yourself, "There he goes again—it's a pity he talks to me in that way. I don't like it, but it's not the end of the world, and I can stand it. Even though what he said is wrong in my opinion, we are fallible humans who have the right to be wrong—I too am not always right—and I choose to not take what he said too seriously," then in all probability you would have felt disappointed and perhaps some mild frustration. These are healthy responses to an unpleasant event, unlike the unhealthy and dysfunctional response of rage.

REBT acknowledges the influence of biological and environmentally learned aspects.

- Humans are born and reared with the capacity to think in both rational and irrational ways. With awareness, people have a choice about how they believe–feel–act (at B), and if they make dysfunctional choices (which many often do), they can reconstruct them and make more functional choices. People can learn (especially with the help of psychotherapy) to see the difference between their functional and dysfunctional choices at B, can learn to correct their dysfunctional beliefs–feelings–behaviors, and, with practice, can habitually come to prefer rational to irrational choices and thereby make themselves less disturbed. It is their biological and learned nature, however, for people to keep falling back to dysfunctional Bs throughout their lives and not to be completely rational or functional. The human condition, as the Buddhists said 2,500 years ago, is to be unenlightened *and* enlightened, never thoroughly and perpetually enlightened.
- There is a clear difference between rational thinking and irrational thinking.

  Rational thinking
  - is based on empirical reality;
  - keeps things in perspective;
  - prefers—as opposed to demands—that things be the way we want them to be;

- is nondamning of self, others, and life; and
- contains high frustration tolerance and creates appropriate and healthy emotions.
  Irrational thinking
- exaggerates, awfulizes, and catastrophizes;
- demands (with shoulds, musts, and oughts) that things be the way one wants them to be;
- judges and damns;
- has low frustration tolerance; and
- creates debilitating and unhealthy negative emotions.

Many therapists, particularly those with psychoanalytic orientations, assume that if clients discover the origins of their disturbances, they will henceforth discover how their neuroses are being perpetuated and how they may be overcome (A. Ellis, 1962; Freud, 1965). REBT disagrees with this assumption and asserts that knowing how people originally learned to behave illogically does not tell us how they maintain their behavior or what they can do to change it. This is especially true because people may suffer from secondary as well as primary disturbances. For example, a person may make herself anxious about not being approved of in an upcoming interview (primary disturbance) and then make herself anxious about the anxiety (secondary disturbance). Understanding the origins of her primary anxiety may not necessarily help her understand and overcome her secondary symptoms. The key to understanding and overcoming disturbance, according to REBT, lies in (a) identifying irrational beliefs and seeing how they cause and maintain unhappiness and disturbance, (b) disputing them, and (c) rethinking and reverbalizing beliefs into rational, self-helping, and life-enhancing forms.

In Al's first major presentation on REBT, given at the American Psychological Association Annual Convention in Chicago on August 31, 1956, he shared some of the major irrational ideas that people believe, explaining that they unthinkingly and consciously reindoctrinate themselves with them again and again, which consequently results in self-defeating and unhealthy emotions and behaviors. Some of these irrational beliefs are instilled by parents and some by the mass media of the culture; some are creatively invented by the believers themselves. They include the following:

- It is a dire necessity to be loved or approved by significant others, rather than rationally concentrating on your own unconditional self-acceptance.
- Certain acts are wrong, wicked, or villainous, and people who perform such acts *must* be damned, in contrast to the rational idea that certain acts are inappropriate and damnable and that people who perform such acts had better be appropriately restrained or attended to but not damned as being totally evil or worthless humans.
- It is terrible, horrible, and catastrophic when things are not the way they *must* be, in contrast to the rational idea that it is too bad when things are not the way you would *like* them to be. You can certainly try to change or control conditions so that they become more satisfactory, but if changing or controlling unfavorable situations is impossible, you had better accept their existence and stop telling yourself how awful they are.
- Unpleasant conditions *must* not exist, and when they do, they directly cause human disturbance, in contrast to the rational belief that much human unhappiness is caused or sustained by the view one takes of things rather than the things themselves.
- If something is or may be dangerous or fearsome, you must be terribly anxious about it, in contrast to the rational idea that if something is, or may be, dangerous or fearsome, you can frankly attend to it as best you can, try to render it nondangerous, and if that cannot be done, you can think of other things and stop telling yourself it absolutely *must* not exist.
- Hassles *must* not exist, and it is easier to avoid them than to face life's difficulties and self-responsibilities, in contrast to rationally thinking that in the long run, the so-called easy way is almost invariably much harder and that it is best to solve most difficult problems by facing them squarely.
- You *need* something or someone stronger or greater than yourself on which to rely, in contrast to the rational idea that it is usually far better,

healthier, and empowering to stand on your own two feet and gain comfort in yourself and confidence in your abilities to meet the difficult circumstances of living.

- You *should* be thoroughly competent, adequate, intelligent, and achieving in all possible respects, in contrast to the rational idea that you had better *do* rather than always need to do *well* and that you can choose to unconditionally accept yourself as a quite imperfect creature who has some human limitations and specific fallibilities.

- Because something once strongly affected your life, it *should* affect you indefinitely, in contrast to the rational idea that you can learn from your past experiences but not be overly attached to or prejudiced by them.

- Others *must* not act the way they do, and you have to change them to act as you would like them to, in contrast to the rational idea that other people's deficiencies are largely *their* problems and that your demanding that they change is unlikely to help them do so unless they choose to change themselves.

- Human happiness can be achieved by inertia and inaction, in contrast to the rational idea that humans tend to be happiest when they think in healthy ways, are actively and vitally absorbed in creative pursuits, and are devoting themselves to people or projects outside themselves.

- You have virtually no control over your emotions and you cannot help feeling certain things, in contrast to the rational belief that you have enormous control over your emotions if you choose to work at disputing and replacing the irrational ideas that create the unhealthy ones.

As you see, the tyranny of the shoulds and musts is inherent in irrational beliefs.

UNCONDITIONAL ACCEPTANCE

According to REBT principles and practices, one can maintain emotional stability and well-being in life (D. J. Ellis, 2015) and what Buddhists call *considerable enlightenment* (Dalai Lama & Cutler, 1998; Sogyal Rinpoche,

1993) when one consistently—not always—acquires the following three important basic philosophies:

- Unconditional self-acceptance (USA). You always—yes, always—accept yourself with your failings. You refuse to do what notable philosopher Alfred Korzybski (1933) urged against your doing—that is, damning your *self*, your entire *being*, for your mistakes. You may make many mistakes, of course, which humans do. However, you remember that you always have other chances and never damn the entire you for any errors.
- Unconditional other-acceptance (UOA). Just as you refuse to damn yourself for your stupidities, you stubbornly refuse to damn other people for theirs. We are all fallible humans. You see how they screw up but do not condemn them as total screw-ups (Korzybski, 1933). You strive to feel compassion for wrongdoers.
- Unconditional life-acceptance (ULA). You see what is wrong, unjust, and immoral in life and—whenever possible—work to improve it. However, you don't conclude that life itself is hopeless and unchangeable. You accept it, when you temporarily can't improve it, as "bad" or "inconvenient" but not as "horrible" and "awful." You optimistically see that it *can* improve—and do your best to improve it, but not desperately or hopelessly.

REBT reminds us that by continuing to work at acquiring USA, UOA, and ULA—especially during difficult times—and by stopping any whining, moaning, and demanding that things be fair, good, and just, although we may not always get what we want, we can learn from the effort and maintain stability. Even when the reality is that life is not easy, we still have ourselves, and many possible enjoyments, when we practice USA, UOA, and ULA.

THE ABC (OR ABCDE) THEORY

The ABC (or ABCDE) theory of REBT clarifies the connection between an *activating event* and its *consequences* by identifying the *beliefs* involved, and it provides the means for replacing irrational beliefs with rational ones through *disputation* and the emergence of *effective* new philosophies. It simplifies the process of illuminating how we self-disturb and shows the way to un-self-disturb. Clients benefit when their therapists teach them the procedure by doing it with them, and individuals benefit from doing it on their own, particularly through writing, in the early days of learning the REBT technique.

A stands for *activating events* or *adversities*. A person clearly identifies what happened.

C stands for *consequences*. They may be both emotional and behavioral.

Although the Bs precede the Cs, when doing the procedure, it is helpful to identify the Cs first and to notice which of the emotional ones are unhealthy negative emotions, such as anxiety, depression, rage, shame, guilt, jealousy, and hurt. REBT does not seek to change healthy negative emotions, such as concern, sadness, disappointment, annoyance, frustration, and regret, because these are often appropriate responses to difficult circumstances and do not debilitate a person as the unhealthy ones can frequently do. In fact, they can be beneficial and motivate a person.

B stands for *beliefs* or *belief system*. People's belief systems include functional or rational beliefs (RBs) and dysfunctional or irrational beliefs (IBs) and include them strongly (emotionally) and behaviorally (activity-wise). Their RBs, as noted earlier, tend to be preferences and wishes (e.g., "I *want* to perform well and be approved of by significant others"), and IBs tend to include absolutistic musts, shoulds, and demands (e.g., "I *should/must/ought to/have to* perform well and be approved by significant others"). It is important to remember that when people want to change their IBs (which lead to self-defeating consequences) to RBs (which lead to self-helping consequences), they had better work on their believing–emoting–behaving and not merely on their believing. This means, more specifically, that they had better vigorously and forcefully (that is, emotively) change their dysfunctional Bs and, at the same time, forcefully and persistently feel and act against them. Why? Because, as already noted, their believing invariably includes their emoting and their behaving and is integrally related to these.

D stands for *disputing*. After distinguishing rational from irrational beliefs, one keeps one's preferences and forms effective and healthy new philosophies. People achieve this by changing their demands through questioning, arguing with, and vigorously disputing them. There are three main forms of disputing and rational questioning:

- Realistic disputing. In this form of disputing, the IBs are challenged by investigating the truth or factual reality behind them. Typical questions that are asked include the following: Why *must* I perform well? Where is the evidence that I *must* be approved by significant others? Where is it written? Is it really awful, terrible, and as bad as it could be? Can I really not stand it?
- Logical disputing. In this form of disputing, the logic underlying the IBs is investigated. Typical questions include the following: Are my beliefs logical? Do they follow from my preferences? Does it follow that if I perform badly and lose approval of others, then that makes me an inadequate person?
- Pragmatic disputing. In this form of disputing, one investigates the pragmatic outcome of holding the IBs. Typical questions include the following: Will holding this belief help me or hurt me? What results will I get if I believe that I absolutely *must* perform well and always be approved of by significant others? Do I want these results?

When people persistently dispute their IBs and retain their RBs, the outcome is *E*, which stands for *effective new philosophies.* These are healthy, functional, and realistic positions from which to perceive oneself, others, and one's world. Examples of effective new philosophies are the following: "No matter how badly I acted, I am not a bad person—just a person who acted badly that time" and "Although some circumstances in my life are difficult and unfortunate at present, that does not mean that the world is all bad or that my whole life is rotten. Nor will these circumstances last forever." At this point, people can create additional and appropriate coping statements.

Enjoying and maintaining healthy preferences and continuing to surrender dysfunctional demands requires ongoing application of REBT techniques. This takes us to the next key concept of REBT.

WORK AND PRACTICE

Work and practice lead to the most lasting of changes and not only to feeling better but also to getting better. In the following pages are several thinking, feeling, and action REBT techniques, which are also described in many other REBT writings. REBT recommends trying the ones that seem most appropriate for the person and the disturbances he or she wishes to be free of. It recommends giving each technique a solid trial. If one doesn't work, it recommends using another, and another, and still another! Even when one technique works, it pushes for trying some of the others as well. REBT recommends using each method many times. Assess and reassess progress (or lack of it). Keep on doing, doing, doing the methods earnestly, forcefully, and vigorously.

THE MULTIMODAL NATURE OF RATIONAL EMOTIVE BEHAVIOR THERAPY

REBT is multimodal—it has created intellectual, affective, and action techniques and has adapted some methods from other therapies, which have been comfortably integrated with the REBT ones.

REBT was pioneering in that it integrated emotive and behavior methods with thinking methods. Cognitive, emotive, and behavioral methods have been used for centuries by philosophers, religious and spiritual leaders, and therapists to help people with disturbances. Many of these techniques were adopted and adapted by therapists such as Pierre Janet (1898), Paul Dubois (1907), and Alfred Adler (1929). When, in the 1950s, these methods were falling into disuse, Albert Ellis and George Kelly (1955) independently revived them, and in the 1960s and 1970s, Aaron Beck (1976), Donald Meichenbaum (1977, 1997), William Glasser (1965),

David Barlow (1988), and others repeated this revival in using many kinds of cognitive behavior therapy.

Following are some of the main REBT cognitive, emotive, and behavioral techniques.

Cognitive Techniques

ABC (or ABCDE) Method for Emotional and Behavioral Disturbance

This method was described earlier in this chapter.

Possible Secondary Symptoms

Possible secondary symptoms include anxiety about anxiety, depression about depression, and so forth. Acknowledge any self-castigation and accept it as failing to be helpful in changing the primary disturbance, but be aware that does not make *you* a failure. Then go back to using the ABC approach to remedy the secondary symptoms.

Assessing the Cost–Benefit Ratio

This relates to one's unconditional acceptance of self, others, and life on an ongoing basis—of one's behaviors and of one's activities in life. Make lists of the plusses and minuses in each case and assess where changes may be beneficial.

Distraction Methods

These include activities such as meditation, yoga, other relaxation techniques, and exercising, which are often palliative and may work for only a while. Although not elegant solutions, they can be helpful in allowing you to step back, refresh, and subsequently assess the issues of disturbance more objectively and helpfully.

Modeling

Albert Bandura (1997) and other psychologists have used modeling to help children and adults to acquire learning skills, and REBT and cognitive behavior therapists have often taught their clients how to use it successfully (J. S. Beck, 1995; A. Ellis, 2001a, 2001b, 2003a, 2003b, 2005b; A. Ellis & Ellis, 2019). Some ways of using this technique are as follows:

- Find people you know who exhibit the attitudes, emotional well-being, and behaviors you aspire to develop and ask them how they do so. Use their relevant thoughts, feelings, and actions to model yours.

- Investigate people you do not know—perhaps famous ones, whether living or dead—and use them as models. Some of our clients felt inspired by hearing the famous story of Epictetus, a Roman slave who warned his master not to tighten the ball and chain on his leg because he might break Epictetus's leg. The master ignored him, tightened the chain, and actually broke the leg. Whereupon, without feeling hurt and angry, Epictetus calmly said, "See, I was right. You broke my leg." His master was so impressed with Epictetus's self-acceptance and lack of anger that he freed him to become the leading Stoic philosopher of Rome. Al incorporated aspects of his philosophy into REBT theory and particularly liked his wise statement, written in the first century AD in *The Enchiridion*: "Men are not disturbed by things, but by the views which they take of them" (p. 54, A. Ellis, 1962). Some of our clients used Epictetus as a model of accepting and unangry demeanor and helped themselves by choosing to act this way more of the time. The actor Christopher Reeve was rendered paralyzed in a horse-riding accident. He used his remaining years of life to campaign for stem-cell research and other causes; he made an impact and was productive despite his severe disabilities (Christopher and Dana Reeve Foundation, 2010). Many consider him a model of acceptance of adversity and of constructive action despite limitations. Many other models of advantageous behaviors and attitudes can be found.

Biblio–Audio–Video Therapies

Books and recorded sources of information on REBT, on some of the other cognitive behavior therapies, and on various life-enhancing philosophies—current and past—may be helpful for repetitively pursuing the rational practices that are appropriate and reinforcing. Talks by Albert Ellis and workshops and interviews by Debbie Joffe Ellis can be viewed on DVDs and on YouTube (see Suggested Readings and Videos). The Systems of Psychotherapy APA series includes the *Rational Emotive Behavior Therapy* DVD, in which I present a clinical demonstration followed by discussion, and the *Rational Emotive Behavior Therapy Over Time* DVD with Ann Vernon.

Talking About Rational Emotive Behavior Therapy With Others

Helping others by using REBT principles with them reinforces its principles. Talking people out of their rigid irrationalities helps people talk themselves out of their own irrationalities. This is particularly applicable in a group therapy setting.

Problem Solving

REBT encourages practical problem solving. This process includes looking at the adversity you face and figuring out action plans worth trying.

Philosophical Discussion

REBT may also include considerable philosophical discussion with clients, students, colleagues, family, and friends.

Emotive–Evocative Techniques

Rational Emotive Imagery

This can be done in a brief period of time each day and is an effective exercise for quickly changing unhealthy negative emotions to healthy ones. It involves cognizing, as using imagery does. In addition to doing this imagery with clients and teaching them to do it on their own, Al and I regularly used it with volunteers from audiences at workshops, and Al particularly used it in his famous Friday Night Workshops for more than 40 years. Both volunteers and audience observers have consistently reported back, as have clients, that it helped them get in touch with, and change, strong dysfunctional feelings (A. Ellis & Joffe, 2002). The approach was created by Maxie Maultsby, Jr., in 1971 after he studied with Al in 1968. A number of therapists have advocated it (A. A. Lazarus, 1997).

Rational emotive imagery helps people vividly experience one of the fundamental concepts of REBT: that when people are faced with adversity, negative emotions are almost always healthy and appropriate when they consist of feelings of sorrow, disappointment, frustration, annoyance, and displeasure. It would actually be aberrant for a person to feel happy or neutral when these events occurred. Having certain negative emotions is fundamental in helping people to deal with an unpleasant reality and motivate themselves to try to change it. The problem is that practically the whole human race can easily transmute the healthy negative feelings of disappointment and regret into disturbed feelings such as anxiety, depression, rage, and self-pity. These are legitimate emotions in the sense that all emotions are legitimate; however, they usually sabotage rather than help people. Therefore, it is preferable that in using rational emotive imagery, one thinks of something that one sees as very unpleasant and strongly feels the kinds of unhealthy, negative feelings that one would frequently experience in reaction to it. The person gets in touch with these feelings, feels them strongly, and then works on changing them to healthy negative feelings by changing his or her thinking about the same unfortunate situation. When individuals have changed their feelings to healthy (rather than unhealthy) negative ones, they are then to keep practicing, preferably at least once a day, for 30 days, until they have trained themselves to experience, automatically or unconsciously, the *healthy* negative feeling whenever they imagine this adversity or when it actually happens. They usually can manage to bring on their healthy negative feelings within 2 or 3 minutes and within a few weeks are usually able to automatically bring them on. Al and I saw many people achieve excellent results in changing dysfunctional anxiety, guilt, depression, and anger over the years.

Shame-Attacking Exercises

This popular emotive–evocative, as well as behavioral, exercise is famous in REBT. It recognizes that shame is suffered by many who wrongly and demandingly tell themselves that they *should* never act in foolish ways or appear foolish, wrong, or stupid to others. When they demand that they *should not* or *must not* have erred, then they feel ashamed, embarrassed, humiliated, or depressed (or any combination of the above). Shame is created from judging one's act *and* oneself—and from the false interpretation that one's deed represents oneself and that when a deed is rotten and worthless, so is the person. This is false. The shame-attacking exercise does not discourage people from assessing the success or failure of what they do but does encourage the removal of self-damning. It consists of doing something one considers shameful and would normally avoid doing—something one would severely put oneself down for doing. An example is wearing "inappropriate" clothing to a formal occasion; while doing this "shameful" act, one works on one's thoughts and emotions so that one doesn't feel embarrassed—one is intentionally doing a foolish thing while focusing on not putting oneself down while doing it. One of the many suggestions Al shared over the years was to yell out the stops in the subway or on a bus while remaining on the vehicle as it moves on from each of these stops. People may stare—an excellent opportunity to practice unconditional self-acceptance and cessation of self-damning!

Strongly Using Coping Statements

Since the early years of REBT, Al and I recommended that clients and members of the public identify and strongly dispute their irrational beliefs and then devise rational coping statements. By the 1970s, cognitive behavior therapists such as Aaron Beck (1976), Donald Meichenbaum (1977), Maxie Maultsby, Jr. (1971), and David Burns (1980) were also encouraging their clients to do so. I have already described how successful disputing leads to healthy coping statements. What makes this emotive is the vigor and strength used while repeating them over and over, so that with time, one is genuinely convinced of the truth and benefit of them. So one forcefully repeats them, choosing relevant coping statements. Some general ones that many find helpful:

- I *can* stand what I don't like. I just don't like it.
- Even if I fail at something, *I* am never, never, never a failure.
- Nothing is *awful*, just inconvenient.

Role-Playing

In therapy, workshops, and group therapy, role-playing can be helpful for evoking disturbing emotions and then disputing the contributing beliefs so as to feel undisturbed. Among friends, relatives, or group therapy members with whom one role-plays, situations considered difficult are enacted. If the situation, for example, is a risky job interview, the role player gives the fearful person a hard time in the interview, and the person wanting to overcome the fear does his or her best to succeed at it. When others are present and observing the role play, they are then invited to critique the interview. Then the role play is tried again. If the person feels anxious during this next role play, he or she and the "interviewer" (as well as any others present) look for the shoulds, oughts, and musts that are creating the anxiety and insecurity. These demands are then vigorously disputed. The goal is to help the person achieve healthful concern but not unhealthy anxiety. Also helpful is reverse role-playing in which another voices the anxiety-creating beliefs and the person who wants to get rid of them persists in disputing and talking the other out of them.

Make Strong Disputing Audio Recordings

In this exercise, a person audio-records some of his or her IBs, such as, "I must always succeed and be approved of by others." The individual then disputes the IBs in the same recording, realistically, logically, and pragmatically, making the disputing as forceful and emotive as possible. The disputing recording can then be listened to with critical friends, who give constructive feedback and note how forceful it is. The individual listens to it over and over again until it feels solidly convincing.

Use of Humor

People are encouraged to keep things in healthy perspective by not taking themselves and others as well as the actions of themselves and others too seriously. Helpful in this regard are the hundreds of rational humorous songs that Al wrote.

Behavioral Techniques

Reading the previous two sections on cognitive and emotive techniques, you may have noticed that there is some overlap of cognitive, emotive, and behavioral—and in the following techniques, which are largely behavioral, you will see overlap again. This reflects a pioneering REBT theme from 1955 that is still emphasized now: Human thinking, feeling, and behaving are integrated and include important aspects of each other.

In Vivo Desensitization

REBT recommends systematized assignments in which one undergoes exposure to uncomfortable situations or in which one does a graduated series of assignments and forces oneself to keep repeating what one is afraid of until the fear disappears (A. Ellis, 2010; A. Ellis & Harper, 1961, 1975, 1997). For example, if one suffers from social anxiety, one may at first just attend a social gathering; at a second occasion, one may talk with one or two people; on the third occasion, one may make more effort to get to know someone there; on the fourth occasion, the person arranges to see a person again on another occasion; and so forth. In this process, people risk doing what they are afraid of and prove to themselves that even if they fail to achieve a goal, they are not failures and can keep trying and surviving, again and again. Over time, with constant repetition of rational coping statements, anxiety, fears, and phobias diminish.

Using Reinforcements

Fred Skinner's (1971) and Joseph Wolpe's (1990) techniques of reinforcement can be used for almost any behavioral methods. For example, if you promise yourself to do some shame-attacking homework but actually reinforce your feelings of shame by refusing to do it, you can reinforce yourself with easy and pleasant tasks, such as listening to music or socializing with your friends, only after you have done your assigned homework. Remember, again, however, that the goal had better be, first, to do the shame-attacks and make it easier (almost routine) to do them but, second, to see philosophically how they particularly foster self-acceptance while one is under fire. If one forces oneself to do the shame-attacks when difficult and critical people are watching, so much the better! One can fight disturbing oneself about one's shaming as well as one's own at the same time.

Using Reinforcing Penalties

Fred Skinner (1971) was opposed to penalizing oneself when assigned shame-attacking and other onerous homework and failing to carry out the assignments. Be that as it may, Al and I have personally found penalties practical and, sometimes, almost the only things that will help one do what one doesn't want to do, as well as strongly encourage one to do it.

Skill Training

REBT specializes in encouraging people to do, as homework, training in skills they want to develop—for example, taking courses in public speaking or assertiveness training, bibliotherapy, and so on.

Relapse Prevention

People are encouraged to take actions that prevent relapse, to accept themselves if they do relapse, and to use self-helping thoughts, feelings, and behaviors if they resume dysfunctional behavior.

Singing Rational Humorous Songs

Already referred to in a previous section, these songs can combat over-seriousness and help keep things in perspective—especially when done loudly and with gusto! A typical song is the following:

I'm Just Wild About Worry
(Lyrics: Albert Ellis; Tune: "I'm Just Wild About Harry," by Eubie Blake)

Oh, I'm just wild about worry
And worry's wild about me!
We're quite a twosome to make life gruesome
And filled with anxiety!
Oh, worry's anguish I curry
And look for its guarantee!

Oh, I'm just wild about worry
And worry's wild about
Never mild about,
Most beguiled about me!

GENERAL SEMANTICS

REBT embraces aspects of general semantics. Some of the main general semantics principles are incorporated in REBT, and as did Alfred Korzybski (the founder of general semantics), Al and I always taught our respective audiences to stop overgeneralizing and to think more sanely—and I continue to teach this. Korzybski (1933) wrote on the "is" of identity, of predication, which encouraged Al from REBT's formative years onward to help clients realize that they do both good and bad neutral things, but that does not make them good, neutral, or bad people. Since its beginning, REBT has taught people to rate not their self or personhood but their acts, deeds, and performances in relation to their goals and purposes. I believe that Korzybski would have endorsed REBT's continual crusading against people's absolutistic, dogmatic, overgeneralized shoulds and musts. He also advocated increasingly using the term *etc.* because he said it facilitates flexibility and gives a greater degree of conditionability in semantic reactions. Korzybski also formulated the REBT concept of secondary symptoms (e.g., anxiety about anxiety) by talking about second-order reactions (e.g., "thinking about thinking," "doubt of doubt," "fear of fear"). He endorsed physico-mathematical methods of thinking (which include accurate observations and the seeking of and reference to objective evidence, both of which make logical evaluations and predictions possible) and said that such methods link science with problems of sanity. He warned that metaphysical terms are not to be trusted and that speculations based on them are misleading or dangerous. In Al's various criticisms of overly mystical and transpersonal ideas and practices in psychotherapy, he expanded on Korzybski's crusading against dangerous kinds of mysticism. The more Al used to think about Korzybski's masterpiece *Science and Sanity* (1933) when he was young, the more he was enthralled by its revolutionary title. For after practicing REBT for several years and trying to assess its effectiveness by using the scientific method to check its results, and after helping hundreds of disturbed people by scientifically, realistically, and logically disputing—at point D in REBT—their neurosis-producing irrational beliefs, he saw that REBT and the other cognitive behavior therapies that dispute people's dysfunctional beliefs tend to show that neurosis and antiscience are similar and that mental health and science distinctly overlap.

HUMANISTIC OUTLOOK

REBT follows a humanistic outlook. REBT, along with many of the cognitive therapies in general, is among the most humanistic of psychological approaches. It deals with people's most uniquely human cognitions and beliefs, rather than looking mainly at stimuli (e.g., early childhood causation), symptoms, and responses. It encourages choice and existential freedom while acknowledging the influence of our biological nature. It is deeply philosophical and encourages rational reeducation and elegant personality-restructuring solutions to emotional disturbances, as opposed to simply focusing on the removal of symptoms. It encourages the development of high frustration tolerance of the individual for his or her human fallibility and frailties, for that of other humans, and for life's challenges. It encourages balance between short-range and long-term hedonism. Most important, it strives to show people how to accept themselves, others, and the world, realistically and unconditionally. It encourages gratitude, compassion, and kindness—toward oneself and toward others. It accepts the world of probability, uncertainty, and disorder, holds no absolutes, and encourages flexibility.

REBT encourages both individuality and sociality. While reminding people of their self-responsibility and the importance of attending to themselves, it also recommends social interest and participating with—and contributing to—others in their community and, when possible, outside of it and to causes in the world at large.

CONCLUSION

REBT is an elegant, enriching, self-empowering, and impactful approach for those who consistently apply and use it. As was Al, I am convinced of this from my personal experiences and my clinical experiences and findings, as well as from research findings. I do not demand that REBT be used to reduce or eliminate suffering and to create greater happiness in the lives of as many as possible, but I most strongly and emphatically would prefer it!

4

The Therapy Process: Primary Change Mechanisms

Rational emotive behavior therapy (REBT) strives to achieve lasting change for clients. Previous chapters have shared basic REBT concepts and techniques and pointed out that it aims to facilitate profound change in the philosophies that create the disturbances people suffer, rather than merely remove symptoms. It acknowledges the tendency to relapse into former dysfunctional behavior after progress has been made, and clients are taught relapse-prevention methods (e.g., regular self-monitoring, disputing any irrational beliefs that may lead to relapse). They also are taught how to accept themselves unconditionally if they do relapse and are encouraged to revert to their self-helping and life-enhancing thoughts, feelings, and behaviors. REBT methods can be described as elegant and efficient because they require relatively little therapeutic time and can be used on an ongoing basis outside of the realm of therapy—at home, at work, and during leisure activities.

http://dx.doi.org/10.1037/0000134-004
Rational Emotive Behavior Therapy, Second Edition, by A. Ellis and D. Joffe Ellis

However, clients and all who use REBT are reminded that some of them may benefit from continuing therapeutic work and practice for years to come. It shows that they have responsibility for their thoughts, feelings, and actions—that they have choice. It shows clients how they have largely created their emotional disturbances, then teaches them how to uncreate them and how to prevent reoccurrence. REBT aims to promote psychoeducational methods that help clients help themselves and that can be given to large numbers of nonclients, and, toward this goal, REBT encourages one and all to use biblio-, audio-, and videotherapy and to attend lectures, workshops, and courses.

CHANGING ABSOLUTISTIC THINKING

The main philosophies behind severe depression, anxiety, hostility, and rage and other dysfunctional states, feelings, thoughts, and behaviors are, according to REBT, a lack of unconditional acceptance of oneself, others, and life. These dysfunctional states are also created by one's insistences, commands, and demands that one absolutely must think, feel, and do better than one is doing and that if one does worse than that at any time— or at least often—one is an inadequate, worthless person who will practically *never* do better and is an unlovable and unworthy mess. Specifically, one strongly believes such absolutistic premises as the following:

- "I absolutely must do well."
- "I absolutely must do very well."
- "I absolutely must do perfectly well."

From these premises, mistaken conclusions are derived, such as

- "I'm *undeserving of any pleasures* if I don't."
- "I'm *no good* if I don't."
- "I'm *completely unlovable* if I don't."
- "I'll *always fail* and be rejected if I don't."
- "I'll be *completely alone* if I don't."
- "I can't enjoy almost *anything* if I don't."
- "I *hardly deserve* to live if I don't."

Notice that having absolutistic premises, such as "I *must* do well at all times and under all conditions," frequently leads to mistaken conclusions that often logically follow from the unrealistic premises. If the premise is that ice cream is poison, the conclusion will be, assuming that one wants to live, to avoid eating it. Why not?

One's absolutistic premises are overgeneralizations, as Alfred Korzybski pointed out in *Science and Sanity* (1933): If one absolutely must perform well, one must *always* do so and in all circumstances, with no exceptions. One's conclusions about one's absolutistic premises are also overgeneralizations: One is *no good, totally undeserving, completely unlovable,* and will *always* feel that one can't enjoy *anything* and hardly deserves to live *at all.* Rather extreme! Moreover, highly unrealistic.

However, people, as Korzybski said, are born and socially raised to generalize and to overgeneralize. We "naturally" tend to do so—and thereby make ourselves, according to REBT, depressed, anxious, enraged, hostile, and so on. Fortunately, being also constructivist, we do not have to make these kinds of absolutistic premises or make "logical" deductions from them. Even if we do so, we can think about their disadvantages and rethink and redo our premises and our conclusions.

REBT teaches how to produce sensible, nonabsolutistic premises and how to make generalized conclusions but not overgeneralize from them. REBT reminds us to be aware and to vigilantly check our premises and conclusions. It encourages the keeping of healthy and realistic wants, desires, goals, and values and the surrendering of absolutistic shoulds, oughts, musts, commands, and demands.

Al saw this and helped himself immensely in 1937, at age 24, with an issue he was having at that time. He was madly in love with Karyl, the woman who was to become his first wife. She was changeable and indecisive, and he was getting nowhere with her. One day she would proclaim her adoration for him, yet another day she would say he was too aesthetic for her and show interest in other men. One midnight after yet another conflicting evening with Karyl, feeling sorely troubled about the seesaw nature of their relationship, he decided to go for a walk around the lake in the Bronx Botanical Gardens on his way home. He wanted to think things over. He realized that his love for Karyl was immense but that it had too much pain attached to it. He thought that maybe it would be better to end the affair and look for a woman who would love him steadily, not intermittently.

Suddenly and significantly, he saw the way out of his dilemma and suffering. He realized that it was not his strong desire for her that created his pain when it was not fulfilled—it was his dire need for her love. He had foolishly believed that she *absolutely must* feel for him the way he felt for her and only that would solve the problem. Nonsense! He then realized that he could, if he wanted to, keep his powerful desire, urge, and love for her and, simultaneously, give up his need, demand, musts, and insistence that she feel exactly the way he did. He could love without needing! He saw clearly that asinine insistence that one *absolutely must* under all conditions always get what one wanted, that one must be loved, and that one should never suffer would only result in anxiety, depression, rage, or some other extreme upset. He saw that persistent happiness could never exist if one held such unrealistic ideas. So in that one 20-minute walk by the lake, he gave up most of his neediness. When he told Karyl, she was impressed, wanted also to achieve that way of loving, and suggested they have an experimental nonneedy marriage! What happened after that is a long story that Al shared in his autobiography (A. Ellis, 2010), but the main message is that since his startling realization and for the rest of his life, he had strong desires, many of which he strove to fulfill, but he rarely, if ever, thought that he absolutely needed what he wanted or that he absolutely must avoid what he abhorred. In later years, this anti-neediness, anti-awfulizing, and anti-*musturbation* (see the Glossary of Key Terms) became solid parts of REBT.

Karen Horney, a liberal non-Freudian psychoanalyst, confirmed Al's view in 1950 when she wrote about the "tyranny of the shoulds." He had revised his idea, even before he read about hers, when he started doing psychotherapy in 1943. Since then, he called it the "tyranny of the musts." No musturbation!

As we persistently practice catching our self-defeating should-ing and musturbation, disputing these irrational beliefs, and consequently creating healthy rational beliefs, healthier habitual ways of thinking replace the unhealthy irrational thinking habits. Over time one can find rational beliefs emerge in response to adverse situations without one's consciously seeking them.

I found this to be the case when a speeding cyclist ran into me on a pedestrian pathway in 2015. When I regained consciousness, my attitude was one of gratitude that the outcome was no worse, and I felt relieved and strangely tranquil that my response was automatically one of calm and steadiness—not one of rage, anxiety, or both (D. J. Ellis, 2015). In fact, research suggests that a grateful outlook may have emotional and interpersonal benefits (Emmons & McCullough, 2003).

DISPUTING RIGID THINKING AND USING RATIONAL COPING PHILOSOPHIES

REBT's many thinking, feeling, and action methods of helping us see and dispute our musts and needs make it, in Arnold Lazarus's (1989, 1997) terms, one of the pioneering multimodal therapies. It shows how to argue out of demands and turn them into mere preferences and then to create antimusturbatory rational coping statements. These have been extensively researched by Richard Lazarus and his associates and have proved to be significantly effective (R. S. Lazarus, 1966; R. S. Lazarus & Folkman, 1984). Similarly, REBT clinical practice and researches have also validated them, and, all told, they have been supported in many studies.

After one has seen and tidied up one's premises and conclusions, it is helpful to write rational coping philosophies to replace them, making sure that they are preferences and desires and not absolutistic musts and shoulds and that they are not overgeneralizations or absolutistic statements. For example, if a person who is feeling depressed rigidly thought, felt, and behaved in a manner indicating that "I absolutely must do well at work and love, because if I don't, I'm no good," some rational coping philosophies could be the following:

- "I'd like very much to do well at work and love, but of course I don't have to do so. If I do poorly, my work and my relationships may fail, but my worth as a person doesn't depend on them because I do scores of things adequately and well and cannot judge my whole being on the basis of some rejections."

- "I did badly this time but may do well in the future."
- "I didn't do *that* badly and can PMA and work at improving." (PMA is a variant of PYA. See the Glossary of Key Terms, this volume.)
- "I'm a fallible human and may often do badly. Tough!"
- "Awfulizing about my bad performances will tend to make them worse, and I can choose not to awfulize."
- "Even if I never succeed at work, I can still be happy in other parts of my life."
- "If I try harder at building good relationships, I'll most likely succeed at building some enjoyable ones."
- "Even if I don't significantly improve at work, I can always accept myself or damn myself for doing badly. I *choose* to accept myself."

Thus, changing unhealthy and irrational philosophies to healthy ones as just described, in addition to using additional cognitive, emotive, and behavioral techniques, is the effective, REBT way to go.

ROLE OF THE THERAPIST–CLIENT RELATIONSHIP

Although REBT certainly acknowledges that a healthy therapist–client relationship can facilitate beneficial change in clients and their disturbances as much research supports (Ivey, Ivey, & Zalaquett, 2018; Lambert, 2013; Norcross & Lambert, 2011; Yager, 2015), REBT does not propose that it is the main agent of change. Although it can be a main change agent, I believe that good therapeutic theory and effective therapeutic technique and skills for implementing it are of greater importance.

If therapists do not adequately relate to their clients, clients may be less willing, or unwilling, to communicate openly or to listen carefully, which lessens the chances of the client's grasping and effectively applying the theory and its techniques. Thus, relating well is an important part of the therapist's method and certainly may contribute to clients "feeling better" during therapy, but it is not, I believe, crucial or even necessary for the longer term "getting better" of many clients.

Certainly, REBT favors building good rapport with clients, uses empathic listening and reflecting of feelings, and strongly encourages helping clients become more aware of themselves and make beneficial changes. At the same time, it acknowledges the dangers of creating a dependent relationship between client and therapist. Such dependence can be harmful for clients who have a dire need for approval, when the therapist's appearance of greatly favoring them may accentuate this need. Similarly, REBT recommends that therapists look at any need they may have for approval from their clients. Such a need may prevent the therapist from using some important REBT techniques, such as disputing clients' irrational beliefs or giving challenging homework. Hence, REBT encourages therapists to look at their motives if they are building overly warm and close relationships with clients for unhealthy reasons (A. Ellis, 1985, 2002).

REBT often invites clients to be active and equal collaborators with the therapist in increasing their awareness and changing themselves. However, it also sees the therapist in the role of a highly active–directive teacher, with greater knowledge about the human personality and its self-disturbing and self-helping tendencies than many clients may have. Thus, the therapist, appropriately, will take the lead in explaining, exploring, interpreting, and disputing clients' dysfunctional beliefs and behaving, as well as in helping them come up with strategies and solutions to the problems they face.

ROLE OF THE THERAPIST

With the goals of therapy largely being to help clients suffer less by teaching them how to disturb themselves less and to enable them to live lives of greater happiness and fulfillment, one of the main roles of an effective therapist is to be a skillful psychoeducator, one who can teach clients

- how they disturb themselves,
- how to undisturb themselves,
- how to create healthy emotions more of the time, and
- how to maintain gains achieved in therapy.

Helping clients feel better is without doubt of benefit. When they feel better, they function better—in the short term. There are many ways clients can feel better. They can distract themselves enjoyably from their problems and disturbances by absorbing themselves in interesting or pleasurable pursuits such as exercise, meditation, yoga, reading, and computer activity. They can also use unhealthy forms of distraction, such as alcohol, drugs, and other such escapes. They may feel better when the therapist expresses kindness, encouragement, optimism, cheerfulness, support, empathy, and acceptance. This does not, however, mean they'll get better, which is more important and, for many, can be more difficult to achieve. Getting better consists of feeling better, experiencing fewer disturbances (emotional, behavioral, and cognitive), making an ongoing effort to prevent recurrence of disturbance, and being able to apply methods to minimize disturbances when new adversities occur.

Thus, an effective REBT therapist patiently and thoroughly teaches clients the main principles of REBT and the main cognitive, behavioral, and emotional methods as appropriate and relevant.

The effective REBT therapist helps clients make the effort to achieve unconditional self-acceptance philosophically, emotionally, and behaviorally. This is a significant part of helping a client get better.

The effective REBT therapist works consistently to achieve and retain unconditional other-acceptance of their clients, especially when clients relapse, resist, or are hindering their progress in other ways. As much as possible, the REBT therapist attempts to practice what he or she preaches and to model healthy behavior. The therapist does his or her best to give clients genuine unconditional other-acceptance.

The effective REBT therapist encourages the client as much as possible. Even if a client relapses or did not do the agreed-upon homework, the therapist will look for, usually find, and express in a genuine and authentic manner something that the client has done or shifted that is positive and life enhancing.

The effective REBT therapist actively, vigorously, forcefully, and directively brings clients' errors—such as irrational thinking, self- and other-disparaging, and other major cognizing faults—to their attention.

The effective REBT therapist does not wait for clients to gain the insights themselves, but when they do, the therapist acknowledges and encourages such progress.

The effective REBT therapist encourages clients to use various psycho-educational resources, such as suitable books, CDs, DVDs, lectures, workshops, courses, and even relevant movies. Homework assignments are given. Clients are reminded frequently that lasting change is achieved by ongoing work and practice. The therapist remembers to check on whether the homework was done, and if it was not, without castigation, he or she explores with the client why it was not and, in particular, any contributing self-defeating thoughts.

Effective REBT therapists listen carefully and thoroughly. It is important and advantageous for them to be creative and experimental, to use stories and parables to help make their points, and to have a good sense of humor and use it. Effective REBT therapists are open-minded and non-dogmatic; they avoid overgeneralizations and other non-REBT language. They have a strong desire to help and motivate the client. They are creative in problem solving and highly ethical. They are able to work on themselves ("Healer, heal thyself") and to practice what they preach as often as possible. They have wide experience and knowledge and high frustration tolerance (HFT); communicate clearly, understandably, and well; and, preferably, enjoy doing therapy.

All these factors are important and helpful, but most important are the therapist's REBT theory and method, which encourage awareness, reflection, philosophizing, and action.

Al was known to use colorful language with clients at times. This was done intentionally, as will be seen later in this chapter in the transcript of his work with Sara, to aid in jolting clients out of rigid thinking and to make his points strongly and memorably. He did not believe that all REBT therapists had to follow his style. However, he did recommend that therapists express themselves in ways that may best help their clients, even if this means stretching comfort boundaries. I myself am no less vigorous or passionate in expression during sessions or teaching demonstrations than my husband was with his clients. However, I have a different tone and manner; I usually do not use the colorful language that he used and have my own way of communicating and using humor. So—as REBT encourages—I stick to its principles and apply them in my unique style.

ROLE OF THE CLIENT

The more solidly a client understands the philosophy and theory of REBT and the more he or she applies the principles and does the homework assignments given by the therapist, the greater and more lasting the changes in his or her life will be. This is particularly the case with ongoing work and practice. A motivated client who is committed to taking action where required is likely to feel better and get better.

Clients are more likely to achieve their realistic therapeutic goals when they are willing to acknowledge their tendencies to self-disturb and do not minimize or deny them and when they admit any difficulties, whether innate or learned, in recognizing and changing dysfunction. They work on accepting themselves unconditionally with or without these difficulties and accept any relapses that may occur. They are most successful in their therapy when they continue to take action.

It is helpful for clients to have realistic expectations about the REBT process and likely outcomes and to embrace the fact that progress will come as a result of their active participation in the process. They accept that magical cures and miracles are unlikely and that they are responsible for their own emotional destinies by making appropriate effort.

Clients who fail to consistently dispute their irrational beliefs are less likely to experience healthy change. Reasons vary and include refusal to do cognitive assignments, poor understanding of the approach and what is required of them, extreme disturbance, grandiosity, laziness, or lack of organization. They may refuse to take responsibility for their unhealthy emotions and refuse to change their actions and beliefs, forcefully and emotively. They may be needy for the approval of others, including their therapist, and resist honest, forthright feedback that is given to them. They may be more severely depressed or otherwise disturbed than are those who do progress, or more stubborn and rebellious. Clients who tend to do poorly in behavioral aspects of REBT tend to succumb to low frustration tolerance, have addictions, and live disorganized lives and may suffer from various psychoses (rather than neuroses).

The REBT approach may be more effective with clients who have a single major symptom than with more seriously disturbed clients. Chronic avoiders are among the more difficult clients; they keep hoping for magical solutions to just happen without any significant self-effort on their part.

Nonetheless, over my years of clinical practice, I have seen even the most "difficult customers" make some progress facilitated by their use of REBT. For example, I have worked with clients with psychoses, such as schizophrenia. When on medication and in touch with "reality," many of the more responsive clients I worked with could understand REBT concepts and especially benefited from developing greater unconditional self-acceptance—fully accepting themselves as worthwhile and fallible humans—including and despite their disability.

It is appropriate for REBT individual therapy to terminate when the client and therapist agree that significant progress has been made and the client is proficient at applying REBT methods on an ongoing basis to maintain therapeutic gains and avoid new disturbances. It is often helpful to schedule some follow-up sessions after the cessation of regular therapy sessions to monitor progress and deal with any remaining obstacles or new issues. It may also be advisable for some clients who terminate individual therapy to enter a term (or longer) of REBT group therapy and to attend REBT workshops, presentations, and courses. Ongoing reading of REBT and other helpful books and materials is also useful.

Many of Al's former individual clients would attend the Friday night workshops and other presentations that Al and I would give. This helped them maintain and reinforce their awareness and application of REBT principles. Today, I continue to give regular workshops in the tradition of my husband, in New York City and in other cities throughout North and South America and in countries around the world.

BRIEF AND LONG-TERM STRATEGIES
AND TECHNIQUES

Brief Therapy

REBT has been demonstrated through countless people over the years since the mid-1950s to be a powerful and very effective approach as a brief therapy. Its simplicity, precision, and elegance (in identifying the problem's root causes and attending to them, rather than seeking methods that bring only short-term relief) have allowed clients who were motivated to make the effort required to facilitate change to not only feel better but also get better, within months, and sometimes within only weeks. When one understands the REBT principles, is willing to be vigilant in applying them (particularly by choosing to be aware of one's thinking and to quickly dispute the thoughts that create the debilitating emotions), and is willing to continue to make such effort, change happens. It takes knowledge of REBT principles and tools, the earnest desire for change, mindful application, and ongoing effort.

When Al originated REBT, it was designed as a therapy that could be effective and brief for many clients. After his experience working as a psychoanalyst from 1947 to 1953, during which he found that most forms of psychoanalysis were too drawn-out, long-winded, and inefficient, Al (with what he called his "gene for efficiency") started using REBT, both briefly and in more prolonged treatment. Clients who are severely disturbed, for biological as well as environmental reasons, usually benefit more from longer term and more intensive treatment, but many individuals who self-disturb or self-neuroticize can be significantly helped in five to 12 sessions and, in some cases, even fewer.

When clients understand the REBT principles of how they disturb themselves, of how they can undisturb themselves, and of how they can choose to maintain healthy thinking, feeling, and behaving, they are well on the way to stability and greater fulfillment. They have learned that they can maintain their gains by continuing to practice REBT principles—and they make the effort to do so. Effective therapy that produces lasting results is a lifelong process, initiated with a therapist and maintained by self-therapy and ongoing effort (and follow-up and refresher sessions when appropriate).

Thus, in effective REBT brief therapy, clients soon grasp that

- their emotional disturbances are largely created as a result of irrational thinking and the tendency to escalate preferences into absolutistic shoulds, oughts, and musts;
- by actively and vigorously disputing their absolutistic demands—while maintaining their preferences—with thinking, feeling, and acting methods, the demands can be changed to healthy preferences;
- dysfunctional thinking, feeling, and actions can easily return, and ongoing effort will be required to prevent that from happening;
- if a relapse occurs, they can unconditionally accept themselves with the relapse, recognizing that it is a human tendency to fall back at times and that all humans are fallible—then they can return to the methods that worked for them before; and
- they had better willingly do "homework" for the rest of their lives.

Al and I often shared with clients one of our famous lines: "Life has inevitable suffering as well as pleasure. By realistically thinking, feeling, and acting to enjoy what you can, and unangrily and unwhiningly accepting painful aspects that cannot be changed, you open yourself to much joy." When remembering this, clients can experience healthy perspective.

In my experience as well as Al's, some clients, usually those who are highly motivated and particularly bright, effected healthy transformations in their lives after only one or two sessions. Many were already quite self-aware and had read a great deal of useful literature, and the REBT seemed to succinctly formulate in easy-to-do form some of what they had already been contemplating. A good number of people familiar with Buddhism, and some of them who practiced it, took quickly and easily to the ABCs of REBT. Some of the similarities between Buddhist and REBT principles were described earlier in this book.

And talk about *brief* therapy: In a study of volunteer clients who took part in live sessions of REBT in front of a public audience (A. Ellis & Joffe, 2002), Al and I learned that 97 of the 100 respondents found their session helpful. The study was based on demonstrations that we gave with volunteers from the audience at our weekly Friday Night Workshops, which were open to members of the public. Volunteers agreed to participate in a 30-minute demonstration with Al, quite a brief time indeed, and their issues and problems were explored using REBT. Many experienced significant insights and beneficial change in just that half hour, and homework was suggested based on what had been done, to be carried out for the following 30 days. It is hoped that they carried out their homework and that they continued to remember REBT principles and to act on them.

Another example of the efficacy of REBT as a brief therapy is seen in the experience of one of my clients. Vanessa benefited immensely from weekly sessions of REBT therapy over 6 months. She had received mainly psychoanalytic therapy for years prior and had not felt significantly better, and a former client of mine suggested to her that she try REBT.

The Case of Vanessa

Vanessa worked in the administration division of an airline company. She was a Caucasian in her mid-30s, tall, slim, attractive, and taking an extended break from work at the time of beginning REBT therapy. She previously had been in therapy for more than 17 years, with a variety of therapists, including psychologists and psychiatrists, as she struggled with anxiety and depression. At the time of beginning REBT therapy she was taking Zoloft and was considering the addition of Abilify (under a psychiatrist's supervision). The bent of her past therapists had been largely psychoanalytical, and she felt that she wasn't getting anywhere with them. She still felt depressed and anxious despite her weekly therapy sessions, and at times her anxiety would escalate to panic states.

Recent issues that seemed to catapult Vanessa into more intense levels of her depression, anxiety, and panic included a breakup the previous year with the man she considered the love of her life and no consequent success when dating men, none of whom she liked much. She felt shy, not good enough, not pretty enough, and self-conscious. At times, she felt hopeless and despondent. She was also desperate to have children and feared that if she didn't meet a love soon, she might never be able to have any children with a mate she loved as she got older. She considered freezing some of her eggs but found the cost of doing so would be too exorbitant. She believed that by her age she should already have found her lifetime partner/mate, as many of her friends had already done, and she felt that she never would. She also was struggling with demanding and critical family members, who were telling her what she should and shouldn't be doing with her life. She also reported perfectionistic tendencies at work and home. She felt that she had no purpose and lost interest in life.

Vanessa's goals in seeking REBT therapy were to overcome anxiety, depression, hopelessness, and perfectionism. As our therapy sessions progressed, additional unhelpful tendencies were exposed, such as obsessive–compulsive tendencies and abysmal self-downing. Attending to these issues became additional therapeutic goals.

Interventions

After taking her history and listening well and expressing care and empathy, I developed rapport with Vanessa and clarified therapeutic goals. I practiced psychoeducation and taught Vanessa the connection between our thinking and emotions and behaviors, that we create our own emotions (as well as the fact that the circumstances and events of our lives are not the cause of them), and that when we think in healthy rational ways we create healthy emotions. I also recommended various articles and a book on REBT.

In therapy, we engaged in occasional reverse role-playing—I would play Vanessa, and she would try to help me catch and dispute my irrational thoughts. We identified her particular irrational beliefs in vivo, during session, and attended to disputing and changing them. I demonstrated unconditional other-acceptance with the goal of providing a model that she could use to apply unconditional self-acceptance. Homework was given each week (we collaborated in choosing what it would be for each new week ahead)—some cognitive, some emotive, and some behavioral activities and applications. This homework included the following:

- REBT Self-Help forms to help her identify, challenge, and replace her shoulds, musts, and absolutistic thinking

- The encouragement to catch her defeatist ideas and dispute them immediately
- Smiling at strangers each day and saying hello to at least one (in a safe place such as at her gym or in Starbucks)
- Writing in a Gratitude Journal daily
- Adopting a humorous view of dates gone wrong
- Developing greater unconditional self-acceptance—reminding herself that life could still have meaning even if (worst-case scenario) she never met a man she loved and did not have children by focusing on other things that she found fulfilling
- Finding absorbing activities
- Reminding herself daily that her worth did not depend on being with a man, having children, or doing "perfectly" well at work and in all activities
- Leaving her bed unmade for some weeks to challenge her need for things to be perfectly neat and observe that the world did not end when things were not done perfectly
- Inviting her to reflect on and write about the fact that her worth as a person did not come from being perfect, or from looking a certain way, or from having talents
- Reminding herself daily that she had worth simply because she was alive
- Reminding herself daily that she could stand the behavior of others that she didn't like—that she simply didn't like it but could stand it

After 6 months of REBT therapy and the fact that she did make the effort to do her homework activities diligently, the changes Vanessa was experiencing were remarkable. Under her psychiatrist's supervision she was being weaned off her medication. She no longer felt intensely hopeless, depressed, and anxious. Her emotions when unhappy events occurred tended to be the healthy negative emotions such as sadness, disappointment, and concern. She dropped her desperation to get the right man, children, and so forth and focused more on the here and now and accepting herself unconditionally. She still desired a partner and family but knew she could create a good life for herself even if they didn't emerge.

She accepted that she creates her emotions and that her circumstances don't create her feelings, and she felt empowered when remembering that. She learned to be less upset when her dates weren't satisfying or if men she felt somewhat interested in didn't follow up for more dates. She no longer let such a circumstance define her worth or attractiveness. She enjoyed her journaling and reflection as well as smiling at others (and enjoying some smiles back) and saying hello to others. Her need for perfection remained a strong focus of her ongoing self-effort; she reported that she was becoming less compulsive but recognized that she had a way to go before being freer of those tendencies. She reported enjoying life more—even when things don't go the way she thinks they "should"; in other words, her attitude dramatically changed. That said, she recognized that she would have to keep making effort to increase and maintain the healthy changes she was enjoying and was willing to do so.

Long-Term Therapy

This section focuses on REBT group therapy because it is an excellent example of the application of REBT therapy that continues on a long-term basis. As already mentioned, clients with greater endogenous disturbances and poor learning skills can benefit more from long-term individual REBT therapy—and from long-term group therapy. In addition, less disadvantaged clients who have significantly benefited from individual therapy may wisely elect to replace it with long-term REBT group therapy. Some clients choose to do both.

THE THERAPY PROCESS

Let's now look at aspects of REBT group therapy. Some clients go directly into group therapy without having had individual sessions; others join group on the recommendation of their therapist while still attending individual sessions or after a period of individual sessions has concluded. Several methods of psychotherapy use group therapy for expediency reasons—because it is more practical and cheaper for the clients and not because it fits in with the theory that ostensibly underlies these methods.

In addition to being a practical fit, REBT group therapy offers empowering and effective help to group members.

REBT basically uses an elegant and educational rather than a medical or psychodynamic model. Consequently, as with most teaching, it is almost inevitable that it be done in group as well as individual sessions. It is usually used in small group sessions, with from eight to 12 clients on a once-a-week basis, but it is done at times with much larger groups, such as a class of 20 or 30 students or a public workshop at which more than 100 people may be present. Its group aspects are also adaptable to audiovisual presentations because it can be taught and practiced with the use of CDs, DVDs, webcasts, live radio and TV presentations, bibliotherapy, programmed instruction, and other forms of mass media presentations. As much as or more than any other contemporary form of psychotherapy, therefore, it is truly group oriented, and frequently the REBT practitioner uses group processes as the method of choice rather than because special circumstances practically force him or her to do so.

In small-scale group therapy of eight to 12 clients, the participants are interested in getting to the roots of their emotional disturbances, understanding the difficulties of the other members of the group, and helping themselves and their fellow group members to (a) rid themselves of their current symptoms and function better in their intrapersonal and interpersonal affairs and (b) minimize their basic disturbability, so that for the rest of their lives, they will tend to feel appropriate rather than inappropriate emotions and to reduce (and preferably remove) the tendency to upset themselves needlessly. In REBT groups, the therapeutic goal is partly symptom removal, but, more important, for each of the members to achieve a profound philosophic change and (more specifically) to accept (although not necessarily like) reality; to give up all kinds of magical thinking; to stop awfulizing, catastrophizing, and demonizing about life's misfortunes and frustrations; to take full responsibility for their own emotional difficulties; and to stop all forms of self-rating and fully and unconditionally accept oneself and others as being fallible and human.

The main goals of REBT group therapy are the same as those of REBT individual therapy: namely, teaching clients that they are responsible for their own emotional upsets or disturbances; that they can change their dysfunctional or debilitating emotions and behavior by changing their irrational beliefs and self-defeating philosophies; and that if they acquire radically new and profoundly held rational belief systems, many may healthfully cope with almost any unfortunate activating events that may arise in their lives and keep themselves, at worst, deeply sorrowful and regretful but not anxious, depressed, or enraged about these activators. Some of the important group-oriented goals and methods that are used in REBT are discussed below.

Because REBT teaches individuals how to accept the existence of suffering and grim circumstances in life and how to change what they can through effort instead of by whining and demandingness, all group members are encouraged to reveal and discourage the presenting individual's perfectionism, rigidity, and demands. Leaders educate members to make suggestions and constructively criticize any self-defeating or unhelpful thoughts, behaviors, and emotions that come up and to learn from them. However, they are taught not to criticize, damn, or feel hopeless about oneself, others, or life itself. Group leaders do their best to model the REBT attitudes and behaviors. All members are also taught to dispute—logically, realistically, pragmatically, and empirically—the disturbance-creating thinking of the other members.

The therapist usually is appropriately active, probing, challenging, confronting, and directive. He or she persistently models rational thinking and appropriate emoting. He or she not only is a trained therapist but also teaches the scientific, or logicoempirical, method to the group members, so that they can apply it effectively to their personal and emotional lives.

Both the therapist and the group consistently give activity-oriented therapy in the session and homework assignments to group members. Some of these assignments (e.g., speaking up in group itself) may be carried out and monitored during the regular sessions. Other assignments (e.g., making social contacts) are to be carried on outside the group but regularly reported and discussed during group sessions. I have observed that such assignments are more effectively given and followed up when given by a group than by an individual therapist.

REBT includes a number of behavioral methods (as already explained earlier), including assertion training, in vivo risk taking, role-playing, and behavior rehearsal, which can partly be done in individual sessions but are more effective in group. Thus, if a member is usually afraid to tell people what he or she thinks of their behavior, he or she may be induced to do so with other group members.

The group deliberately encourages observing emotions and behaviors rather than obtaining information through the client's secondhand reports. Angry or anxious individuals, who might feel at home with an individual therapist and hide their feelings in therapy, can often reveal much in group, where they interact with several of their peers.

In REBT, some clients fill out written homework report forms and give them to the therapist to go over. In group sessions, a few homework forms are often read and corrected so that all the members of the group, and not merely the individual handing in the form, may be helped to see specifically what unhealthy negative emotional consequence was experienced (at point C); what activating events occurred to spark it (at point A), what rational and irrational beliefs the individual told himself or herself (at point B) to create the dysfunctional consequences, and what kind of effective disputing could be done (at point D) to minimize or eradicate the irrational beliefs that led to the self-defeating consequences. By hearing about other group members' main problems and how they dealt with them on the homework report, clients are helped to use these reports more efficiently themselves.

Individuals receive valuable feedback from the group as to how they malfunction and what they are probably foolishly telling themselves to create their disturbances. They also learn to view others and to give feedback. More important, they gain practice in talking themselves out of their irrational beliefs and therefore in consciously and unconsciously talking themselves out of their own self-defeating irrational beliefs.

One main purpose of REBT group sessions is to offer members a wider range of possible solutions to their problems than they might normally receive in individual sessions. Of 10 people present at a given session, one may finally zero in on a presenter's central problem (after several others have failed), and another may offer an elegant solution to it (after various ineffectual, inelegant, symptom-focused solutions have hitherto been offered). Whereas a single would-be helper may give up on a difficult issue (or person), some group members may persist and finally prove to be quite helpful.

Revealing intimate problems to a group of people may itself be therapeutic for the client. In regular REBT small-group therapy, he or she discloses many ordinarily usually hidden events and feelings to a dozen or so peers. In REBT public workshops, individuals may reveal themselves to a hundred or more people. Especially if they are usually shy and inhibited, this kind of disclosure may be a most useful risk-taking experience, which the therapist will often emphasize by showing the inhibited person that he or she has opened up and actually received little, if any, criticism or an attack that he or she predicted. Further, even if one is disapproved or laughed at, one can still accept oneself and find this censure *unfortunate* rather than *awful.*

Group members are of all ages, usually ranging from about 20 to 70 years old, and include all kinds of diagnostic categories. Groups usually have a fairly equal number of males and females or may intentionally include one gender only. After a member joins a group, he or she may have concomitant individual therapy sessions regularly or irregularly. Most group members choose to have them irregularly and therefore mainly learn the principles and practices of REBT in the course of the group process. Clients who are distinctly shy or who have problems relating to others are particularly encouraged to join a group because working out their difficulties with their peers may be better for them than only working with an individual therapist (who has a particular role with them and therefore is not representative of the people they associate with in real life).

All groups are open-ended. That is, once a member joins, he or she can attend group for a minimum of 6 weeks and then (after giving 2 weeks' notice) drop out at any time. Those who drop out are usually soon replaced by new members. When a member joins, he or she comes into a group that is filled mostly with long-term members who have been in attendance for several months to some years and who help teach some of the "ropes" of

REBT, during regular sessions, after sessions, and in private contacts that they may have during the week. New members are also prepared for the group process by (a) having had one or more individual REBT sessions, (b) having read various books on REBT, and (c) having attended workshops and lectures.

REBT group therapy has some disadvantages and limitations, especially when compared with more individualized REBT processes. In small-group procedures, for example, group members can easily, out of overzealousness and ignorance, mislead other members and at times even present them with harmful directives and views. They can give poor or inelegant solutions, for example, continuing to show a disturbed person the practical methods one can use to make oneself more successful in life, rather than what deeper philosophic changes one can make in disturbance-creating outlooks.

Some difficult and even some well-intentioned group members can waste time in irrelevancies. Some may try to dominate, neglect doing homework assignments, lead the problem presenter "down the garden path," or sidetrack and defuse some of the therapist's main points. Some may hold back because they inordinately look for the approval of other group members; others bring out their own and others' minor instead of major difficulties and otherwise get off on various nontherapeutic limbs. Group members can also bombard a presenter with so many and such powerful suggestions that he or she feels overwhelmed. They can give poor homework assignments or keep presenting so many new problems that old assignments are not sufficiently checked up on. They can allow a member, if the therapist does not actively intervene, to get away with minimal participation and hence make minimal change in his or her disordered behavior. They can become overly frustrated and hostile and can irrationally condemn a participant for his or her symptoms or continuing resistance to working at giving up those symptoms. The well-trained REBT group therapist is vigilant about attending to any of these occurrences and brings the group back on track. REBT group therapy, consequently, is hardly a panacea for all ills, nor is it suitable for all individuals who feel emotionally disturbed and come for help. Some clients are not ready for it and would better continue with individual REBT before entering a group. Others, such as some compulsive talkers or individuals with hypomania, may benefit considerably from group work but can be too disruptive and require too much monitoring and training. Hence, it may be best to exclude them and have them work out their problems in other modes of treatment. However, as did Al, I have always believed that many disturbed clients can benefit as much, and probably more, from group therapy than from individual treatment alone.

To conclude this section on brief and long-term strategies and techniques, I remind readers about REBT's goals of helping people not merely to feel better but to get better for the long term. Hence, both short- and long-term clients are encouraged and taught how to maintain and enhance their REBT gains after they leave therapy and are urged not to hesitate to return for booster individual sessions or to rejoin their therapy group if they backslide, relapse, or think they are progressing too slowly.

Maintaining Therapeutic Gains

The effective REBT therapist offers a number of recommendations to clients for maintenance and enhancement.

Clients may remind themselves, when they improve and then fall back and experience old feelings of anxiety, depression, or self-downing, of the thoughts, feelings, and behaviors they successfully changed in the past to bring about their improvement then. If they again feel depressed, I recommend thinking back to how they previously used REBT to make themselves undepressed. As described earlier in this chapter, the effective therapist will focus on and encourage that which a client is doing or has done that is positive and healthy and that restores hope.

I recommend that they keep thinking rational beliefs or using coping statements, such as "I *can* stand what I don't like" or "I may have failed at this pursuit, but *I* am never a failure. I can keep trying and can learn from the experience."

I recommend they keep seeking, discovering, disputing, and challenging irrational beliefs with which they are once again upsetting themselves.

I recommend that they keep forcefully and persistently disputing their irrational beliefs whenever they see that they are letting them creep back in again, realizing that even when they do not actively hold them, they may arise once more. This is the time to bring those beliefs to their awareness and preventively—and vigorously!—dispute them.

I recommend that they keep risking and doing things that they irrationally fear or dread. After they have partly overcome one of their irrational fears, they can keep acting against it on a regular basis. If they feel uncomfortable in forcing themselves to do things that they are afraid of doing for unrealistic reasons, they had better not allow themselves to avoid doing them, or they will preserve their discomfort forever. Though they may feel intensely uncomfortable as they continue to work to eradicate irrational fears, they can look forward to feeling less anxious, or unanxious, and comfortable later.

I recommend that they work on clearly seeing the real difference between healthy negative feelings, such as sorrow, regret, and frustration, when they do not get some of the important things they want and unhealthy negative feelings, such as depression, anxiety, self-hatred, and self-pity.

I recommend that whenever they feel overconcerned (panicked) or unduly miserable (depressed), they acknowledge they are having a statistically normal but psychologically unhealthy feeling and that they are mainly bringing it on themselves with some dogmatic should, ought, or must.

I frequently remind and urge them to remember that they are capable of changing their unhealthy (demanding) feelings back into healthy (or preferential) ones. They can take their depressed feelings and work on them until they only feel sorry and regretful. They can take their anxious feelings and work on them until they only feel concerned and apprehensive. They can use rational emotive imagery (REI) to imagine unpleasant activating events vividly even before they happen. In using REI they allow themselves to feel unhealthily upset (anxious, depressed, enraged, or self-downing) as they imagine those events, then work to change the unhealthy emotions by using rational thoughts to create healthy negative emotions (concern, sorrow, annoyance, or regret) as they keep imagining some of the worst things happening. I remind them not to give up until they actually do change their feelings.

I recommend they avoid self-defeating procrastination and do unpleasant but beneficial tasks fast—today! To minimize procrastination, they can reward themselves with enjoyable rewards—only *after* they have performed the tasks that they easily avoid. If that doesn't work, they can penalize themselves after every time they procrastinate.

I recommend demonstrating to themselves that it can be an absorbing challenge and something of an adventure to maintain their emotional health and to keep reasonably happy no matter what kind of misfortunes arise. I suggest making it a priority to uproot and remove misery, making it something they are utterly determined to work steadily at achieving. They almost always have some choice about how they think, feel, and behave.

I remind clients to keep using the three main insights of REBT: (a) They largely *choose* to disturb themselves about the unpleasant events of their lives, although they may be encouraged to do so by external happenings and social learning. (b) They mainly feel the way they think. (c) When obnoxious and frustrating things happen to them at point A (activating event or adversities), they consciously or unconsciously select rational beliefs that lead them to feel sad and regretful, and they also select irrational beliefs that lead them to feel anxious, depressed, and self-hating.

I remind them that no matter how or when they acquired their irrational beliefs and their self-sabotaging habits, they now, in the present, choose to maintain them, and that is why they are disturbed. Their past history and present life conditions may importantly affect them, but they don't disturb them. Their present philosophy is the main contributor to their current disturbance.

I remind them that there is no magical way for them to change their personality or their strong tendencies to upset themselves needlessly. Basic personality change requires persistent work and practice to alter irrational beliefs, unhealthy feelings, and self-destructive behaviors.

I suggest they look for personal pleasures and enjoyments and other absorbing interests and make a major life goal the achievement of not only emotional health but also real enjoyment.

I encourage them to work for worthwhile causes and to help other people.

I suggest they try to keep in touch with several other people who know something about REBT and practice using REBT with others. The more often they use it with others and are able to see what their irrational beliefs are and to try to talk them out of their self-defeating ideas, the better they will be able to understand the main principles of REBT and use them with themselves. When they see other people acting irrationally and in a disturbed manner, they can try to figure out—with or without talking to them about it—what their main irrational beliefs are and how these could be actively and vigorously disputed.

When in REBT individual or group therapy, they can record many sessions and listen to these carefully between sessions, so that some of the ideas learned in therapy sink in. After therapy has ended, from time to time these recordings can be played back as reminders of how to deal with some old problems or new ones that may arise. They can also keep reading rational writings.

Regarding dealing with relapse and backsliding, I recommend people accept their backsliding as normal, as something that happens to almost all people who at first improve emotionally and then fall back. It is part of human fallibility. I recommend they don't make themselves ashamed when some old symptoms return or think that it is weak to seek some additional sessions of therapy or to talk to friends about renewed problems.

Self-defeating behavior can be seen as bad and unfortunate, but they can refuse to put themselves down for engaging in this behavior. They can use the highly important REBT principle of refraining from rating oneself or one's being and of measuring only one's acts, deeds, and traits. They are always people who act well or badly—but never are "good" or "bad" people. No matter how much they fall back and bring on old disturbances again, they can work at fully accepting themselves with this unfortunate or weak behavior and then try—and keep trying—to change the behavior.

They can go back to the ABCs of REBT and clearly see what they did to fall back to their old symptoms and dispute irrational ideas with vigor.

They can keep looking for, finding, and actively and vigorously disputing irrational beliefs into which they have once again relapsed and that are now contributing to their feeling anxious or depressed, over and over, until they build intellectual and emotional muscle.

They can keep doing it until they are convinced of their rational answers and until feelings of disturbance truly disappear. Then they can do the same thing many, many times, until their new E (effective new philosophy) becomes solid and habitual, which it almost always will if they keep working at it and thinking it through.

Convincing themselves lightly or "intellectually" of their new effective philosophy or rational beliefs will not help much or persist long. They had better convince themselves strongly and vigorously and do so many times.

People who continue to make an effort to maintain awareness of their backsliding tendencies and who desire to keep on progressing benefit from frequently reminding themselves of the three main kinds of irrational beliefs:

- "I *must* do well and *have to* be approved of by people whom I find important." This belief leads one to feel anxious, depressed, and self-hating and to avoid doing things at which one may fail or relationships that may not turn out well.
- "Other people *must* treat me fairly and nicely!" This belief contributes to one feeling angry, furious, violent, and overly rebellious.
- "The conditions under which I live *must* be comfortable and free from major hassles!" This belief tends to produce feelings of low frustration tolerance and self-pity and sometimes anger and depression.

Clients would do well to recognize that when they use any one of these three absolutistic musts or any of the innumerable variations on them, they derive other irrational conclusions from them, such as the following:

- "Because I am not doing as well as I *must*, I am an incompetent worthless individual!" (self-downing)
- "Because I am not being approved by people whom I find important, as I *have to* be, it's *awful* and *terrible!*" (awfulizing)
- "Because others are not treating me as fairly and as nicely as they *absolutely should*, they are utterly rotten people and deserve to be damned!" (damnation)
- "Because the conditions under which I live are not that comfortable, and because my life has several major hassles, as it *must* not have, I can't stand it! My life is a horror!" (can't-stand-it-itis)

- "Because I have failed and been rejected as I absolutely *ought not* have been, I'll *always* fail and *never* get accepted, as I *must* be! My life will be hopeless and joyless forever!" (overgeneralizing)

Clients can work at seeing that these irrational beliefs are part of a general repertoire of thoughts and feelings, that they bring them to many kinds of situations, and that in most cases in which they feel seriously upset and act in a self-defeating manner, they are consciously or unconsciously sneaking in one or more of these irrational beliefs. Consequently, if they reduce them in one area and are still emotionally disturbed about something else, they can use the same REBT principles to discover irrational beliefs in the new area and minimize them there.

Clients had better repeatedly show themselves that they normally will not disturb themselves and remain disturbed if they abandon their absolute shoulds, oughts, and musts and consistently replace them with flexible and unrigid (although still strong) desires and preferences. They benefit from reminding themselves that their irrational beliefs are self-defeating and do not conform to social reality and deny the fact of human fallibility; their beliefs are illogical—and clients had better keep on disputing them and replace them with rational, realistic, pragmatic, and logical thinking.

Finally, it is of great benefit and a healthy motivating force to have life-enhancing goals, check on their progress, revise them at times, and create new ones when the former ones have been achieved. All the while, clients can strive to continue to deepen the use and frequency of REBT principles and practice.

APPLICATION OF REBT TO VARIOUS DISORDERS, ISSUES, AND CLIENTS

As was true with Vanessa's case, the case of Sara, which is presented later, shows that typically clients have more than one issue or disturbance. Nonetheless, the change techniques and mechanisms of REBT apply remarkably well to the variety and diversity of human issues and conditions, some of which are presented here.

Let us now see some applications of the REBT approach to an assortment of issues and clients.

Anxiety Disorders

The therapeutic answer to much of what causes people's anxiety is to encourage them to keep any and all of their healthy desires for success, approval, and comfort and to refuse, strongly, stubbornly, and vigorously, to escalate them into harmful, self-defeating, and grandiose demands (A. Ellis, 1998, 1999).

One of the main unhealthy emotions that people seek help with is anxiety. Al and I estimated that anxietizing may be one of, if not the, main cognitive–emotive–behavioral disorders, with depression a close second. We found that most anxiety, particularly performance anxiety, stems from clients *demanding* that they do well and be approved of by others. *Preferring* that they do well and gain approval would be fine and may motivate appropriate action for attaining such a goal. However, when there is a demand, insistence, or dire need, anxiety (often with depression) results. In a therapy session, the therapist will identify the beliefs (demands) that lead to anxiety, teach the client how to dispute and replace them, and help the client retain his or her desires for success and approval without escalating the desires into harmful demandingness.

My client Marguerite suffered from severe anxiety. An African American counseling student in her 40s, she felt terrified that she would not get her term paper in on time and felt that even if she did, it would be substandard and not as good as the papers written by her younger fellow students. She felt anxious that she might fail and that if she did, her husband would criticize her and give her a hard time about wasting time and money in going back to college. She feared that in fact she was not "good enough" and that if she failed, it would prove it and that she would be a "nothing" forever.

Her goals in seeking therapy were to feel less anxious and to get her work done, for the anxiety was having a paralyzing effect on her. She would intend to work on her paper, then tell herself she'd never get it done on time, then would find other things to do to avoid the discomfort of effort and not doing well enough at it. Then she would feel more anxious—and then feel anxiety about that (secondary anxiety).

My therapeutic goals for Marguerite were

- to help her accept herself with her anxiety (attending to the secondary symptom);
- to encourage her to accept that anxietizing is a tendency common to many—a part of the human condition;
- to teach her the principles of REBT, emphasizing her ability—if she chose to use it—to work on changing her disabling anxiety to healthy concern, when appropriate;
- to help her identify the irrational beliefs that were leading to her experience of anxiety and self-downing and to her anxiety about her anxiety;
- to give her homework—ongoing tasks and activities to help her overcome her anxiety and maintain her gains as they were achieved—and to remind her that for her positive change to be lasting, ongoing work and practice was required; and
- to help instill the *desire* (not *need*) to do well and be approved and to maintain that *want* while refusing to escalate it into a disabling *demand*.

Some of Marguerite's main irrational beliefs were as follows:

- "I shouldn't be anxious." "I must do well and get my paper in on time."
- "If I don't, it will be awful, and I couldn't stand the shame and humiliation of failing to do what I *should* (i.e., do well and get it done on time)." "If other students do well, and I don't, they will think I'm a loser and too old. And I *should* be able to do better than they do." "My professor will think I'm stupid, and I'll feel too embarrassed to talk with him."
- "I must do at least as well, if not better, than others, to prove myself as a capable and worthwhile person."
- "My husband shouldn't criticize and think poorly of me, and if he does, it means he doesn't love me the way he should. If he rejects and leaves me, that's too awful to even imagine. I couldn't stand his leaving me."

- "If I fail by not achieving what I set out to do, it would prove I'm 'not good enough,' a real 'failure,' which my mother used to tell me I was—over and over again—when I was a child."

Marguerite felt highly motivated to change. She was tired of the painful anxiety and could see how it was harmful to her. With her desire to work as a counselor one day, she realized she'd better get over her disturbances if she wanted to be most effective with her future clients.

With my help, she disputed her irrational ideas realistically, logically, and empirically. She came to see that her irrational beliefs were hurting, not helping, her and that they were unrealistic and did not follow from her preferences. She saw that she was torturing herself unnecessarily. She understood that even if—worst-case scenario—she failed to get the paper in on time or to do well enough, it didn't make her a failure, but just a person who failed at that task. She acknowledged that she was successful at most of the facets of motherhood, at painting, at singing, and in many other things. After I told her of the philosophy of Alfred Korzybski, she accepted that she was not what she did, and her performance, whether good or bad, did not make her a good or bad person or define her worth. Demanding that she do better than other students was going to not only add to her self-made pressure but also increase her anxiety. She saw that she was severely limiting herself by needing approval from others—and feeling ashamed if she thought she didn't have it. She realized that her demanding that her husband be supportive, noncritical, and ever-approving was not going to result in her receiving these things from him; if anything, it would contribute to his acting more in opposite ways to what she desired. She realized that throughout their marriage, her unrealistic and utopian ideas of how he *should* be often alienated him. She saw how her "needing" to never be without him was contributing to her anxiety as well.

Her homework assignments included catching herself when she was demanding and changing that to preferring; pushing herself to do "imperfect" work on her papers without "needing" to do better than others and without "needing" necessarily to enjoy doing the work; and working on not needing approval from others—be it her husband, me (her therapist), her professor, other students, or the king of Siam! She was encouraged to do a shame-attacking exercise, risking disapproval from others, to help her work on unconditionally accepting herself, no matter what others thought. So she wore one red shoe and one cream-colored shoe to college one day. Whenever anyone looked at her strangely, she felt uncomfortable but would tell herself, "So what. I don't *need* their approval, even if I'd prefer it." By the end of the day, she felt quite at ease with her odd shoes, seeing that nothing disastrous happened and that actually very few people seemed to notice or care anyway. She regularly and consistently would tell herself rational coping statements such as, "I *can* stand what I don't like"; "I accept myself, just because I'm alive and kicking, whether or not others do"; "I cannot be a failure. If I fail *at* something, I'll learn from it and keep going. My failing (or succeeding) doesn't make me a failure (or a success)."

After only 12 sessions of REBT, Marguerite felt remarkably transformed. Although she still felt some concern about meeting deadlines and doing well, she no longer "had to" meet them and do well to feel OK about herself. In the absence of the debilitating anxiety, she was getting a lot more work done, and she actually enjoyed some of it. She felt a sense of freedom in not *needing* approval from others, and her relationship with her husband improved—largely due to her newfound lack of neediness and demandingness. Her therapy goals were achieved—and more. She understood that relapse might occur and she knew not to put herself down if that happened but to get back to vigorous application of REBT methods.

As many therapists have experienced, clients do not always appear before them with clear-cut goals, as Marguerite had done. Often a therapist will work on helping a client, who may be experiencing more than one disturbance, to clarify goals and issues.

What follows is a transcript of a session that Al did with Sara, a 25-year-old single, White, Jewish woman (Wedding & Corsini, 2019).[1] It includes some confronting and colorful language, which he used with clients, when appropriate, to jolt them out of their habitual ways of rigid thinking and to make what he told them more memorable.

---

[1]From *Current Psychotherapies* (11th ed., p. 176–181), by D. Wedding and R. J. Corsini, 2019, Boston, MA: Cengage. Copyright 2019 by Cengage Learning, Inc. Reprinted with permission.

Sara worked as the head of a computer programming section of a firm and, without any traumatic or violent history, was very insecure and self-denigrating.

T-1: What would you want to start on first?

C-1: I don't know. I'm petrified at the moment!

T-2: You're petrified—of what?

C-2: Of you!

T-3: No, surely not of me—perhaps of yourself.

C-3: [Laughs nervously.]

T-4: Because of what I am going to do to you?

C-4: Right! You are threatening me, I guess.

T-5: But how? What am I doing? Obviously, I'm not going to take a knife and stab you. Now, in what way am I threatening you?

C-5: I guess I'm afraid, perhaps, of what I'm going to find out—about me.

T-6: Well, so let's suppose you find out something dreadful about you—that you're thinking foolishly or something. Now why would that be awful?

C-6: Because I, I guess I'm the most important thing to me at the moment.

T-7: No, I don't think that's the answer. It's, I believe, the opposite! You're really the least important thing to you. You are prepared to beat yourself over the head if I tell you that you're acting foolishly. If you were not a self-blamer, then you wouldn't care what I said. It would be important to you—but you'd just go around correcting it. But if I tell you something really negative about you, you're going to beat yourself mercilessly. Aren't you?

C-7: Yes, I generally do.

T-8: All right. So perhaps that's what you're really afraid of. You're not afraid of me. You're afraid of your own self-criticism.

C-8: [Sighs] All right.

T-9: So why do you have to criticize yourself? Suppose I find you're the worst person I ever met? Let's just suppose that. All right, now *why* would you have to criticize yourself?

C-9: [Pause] I'd have to. I don't know any other behavior pattern, I guess, in this point of time. I always do. I guess I think I'm just a shit.

T-10: Yeah. But that, that isn't so. If you don't know how to ski or swim, you could learn. You can also learn not to condemn yourself, no matter what you do.

C-10: I don't know.

T-11: Well, the answer is: You don't know how.

C-11: Perhaps.

T-12: I get the impression you're saying, "I *have* to berate myself if I do something wrong." Because isn't that where your depression comes from?

C-12: Yes, I guess so. [Silence]

T-13: Now, what are you *mainly* putting yourself down for right now?

C-13: I don't seem quite able, in this point of time, to break it down very neatly. That form [that our clinic gets clients to fill out before their sessions] gave me a great deal of trouble. Because my tendency is to say *everything*, I want to change everything; I'm depressed about everything, etc.

T-14: Give me a couple of things, for example.

C-14: What I'm depressed about? I, uh, don't know that I have any purpose in life. I don't know what I—what I am. And I don't know in what direction I'm going.

T-15: Yeah, but that's—so you're saying, "I'm ignorant!" [Client nods.] Well, what's so awful about being ignorant? It's too bad you're ignorant. It would be nicer if you weren't—if you *had* a purpose and *knew* where you were going. But just let's suppose the worst: for the rest of your life you didn't have a purpose and you stayed this way. Let's suppose that. Now, why would *you* be so bad?

C-15: Because everyone *should* have a purpose!

T-16: Where did you get the *should*?

C-16: 'Cause it's what I believe in. [Silence]

T-17: I know. But think about it for a minute. You're obviously a bright woman. Now, where did that *should* come from?

C-17: I, I don't know! I'm not thinking clearly at the moment. I'm too nervous! I'm sorry.

T-18: Well, but you *can* think clearly. Are you now saying, "Oh, it's hopeless! I can't think clearly. What a shit I am for not thinking clearly!" You see: You're blaming yourself for *that*.

[From C-18 to C-26 the client upsets herself about not reacting well to the session, but the therapist shows her that this is not overly important and calms her down.]

C-27: I can't imagine existing, uh, or that there would be any reason for existing without a purpose!

T-28: No, but the vast majority of human beings don't have much purpose.

C-28: [Angrily] All right, then, I should not feel bad about it.

T-29: No, no, no! Wait a minute, now. You just *jumped*. [Laughs] You jumped from one extreme to another! You see, you said a sane sentence and an *insane* sentence. Now, if we could get you to separate the two—which you're perfectly able to do—you would solve the problem. What you really mean is, "It *would be better* if I had a purpose. Because I'd be happier." Right?

C-29: Yes.

T-30: But then you magically jump to "Therefore I *should*!" Now do you see the difference between "It *would be better* if I had a purpose" and "I *should*, I *must*, I've *got* to!"?

C-30: Yes, I do.

T-31: Well, what's the difference?

C-31: [Laughs] I just said that to agree with you!

T-32: Yes! See, that won't be any good. We could go on that way forever, and you'll agree with me, and I'll say, "Oh, what a great woman! She agrees with me." And then you'll go out of here as nutty as you were before!

C-32: [Laughs, this time with genuine appreciation and good humor]

T-33: You're perfectly able, as I said, to think—to stop giving up. That's what you've done most of your life. That's why you're disturbed. Because you refuse to think. And let's go over it again: "It would be better if I had a purpose in life; if I weren't depressed, etc., etc. If I had a good, nice, enjoyable purpose." We could give reasons why it would be better. "It's fairly obvious why it would be better!" Now, why is that a magical statement, that "I *should* do what would be better?"

C-33: You mean, why do I feel that way?

T-34: No, no. It's a belief. You feel that way because you believe that way.

C-34: Yes.

T-35: If you believed you were a kangaroo, you'd be hopping around and you'd *feel* like a kangaroo. Whatever you *believe*, you feel. Feelings largely come from your beliefs. Now, I'm temporarily forgetting about your feelings, because we really can't change feelings without changing beliefs. So I'm showing you; you have two beliefs—or two feelings, if you want to call them that. One, "It would be better if I had a purpose in life." Do you agree? [Client nods.] Now that's perfectly reasonable. That's quite true. We could prove it. Two, "Therefore I *should do* what would be better." Now those are two different statements. They may seem the same, but they're vastly different. Now, the first one, as I said, is sane. Because we could prove it. It's related to reality. We can list the advantages of having a purpose—for almost anybody, not just for you.

C-35: [Calm now, and listening intently to T's explanation] Uh-huh.

T-36: But the second one, "Therefore I *should* do what would be better," is crazy. Now why is that crazy?

C-36: I can't accept it as a crazy statement.

T-37: Because who said you *should*?

C-37: I don't know where it all began! Somebody said it.

T-38: I know, but I say whoever said it was screwy!

C-38: [Laughs] All right.

T-39: How could the world possibly have a *should*?

C-39: Well, it does.

T-40: But it *doesn't*! You see, that's what emotional disturbance is: believing in *should, oughts,* and *musts* instead of *it would be betters.* That's exactly what makes people neurotic! Suppose you said to yourself, "I wish I had a dollar in my pocket right now," and you had only ninety cents. How would you feel?

C-40: Not particularly upset.

T-41: Yes, you'd be a little disappointed. *It would be better* to have a dollar. But now suppose you said, "I *should,* I *must have* a dollar in my pocket at all times," and you found you had only 90 cents. Now, how would you feel?

C-41: Then I would be terribly upset, following your line of reasoning.

T-42: But not because you had only 90 cents.

C-42: Because I thought I *should* have a dollar.

T-43: THAT'S RIGHT! The *should.* And what's more, let's just go one step further. Suppose you said, "I must have a dollar in my pocket at all times." And you found you had a dollar and 10 cents. Now how would you feel?

C-43: Superb, I guess!

T-44: No—anxious!

C-44: [Laughs] You mean I'd be guilty: "What was I doing with the extra money?"

T-45: No.

C-45: I'm sorry, I'm not following you. I—

T-46: Because you're not *thinking*. Think for a minute. Why, if you said, "I *must* have a dollar, I *should* have a dollar," and you had a dollar and 10 cents, would you still be anxious? *Anybody* would be. Now why would anybody be anxious if they were saying, "I've got to have a dollar!" and they found they had a dollar and 10 cents?

C-46: Because it violated their *should*. It violated their rule of what they thought was right, I guess.

T-47: Well, not at the moment. But they could easily lose 20 cents.

C-47: Oh! Well.

T-48: Yeah! They'd still be anxious. You see, because *must* means, "At *all* times I must—"

C-48: Oh, I see what you mean! All right. I see what you mean. They could easily lose some of the money and would therefore feel insecure.

T-49: Yeah. Most anxiety comes from *musts*.

C-49: [Long silence] Why do you create such an anxiety-ridden situation initially for someone?

T-50: I don't think I do. I see hundreds of people and you're one of the few who *makes* this so anxiety-provoking for yourself. The others may do it mildly, but you're making it very anxiety-provoking. Which just shows that you may carry *must* into *everything*, including this situation. Most people come in here very relieved. They finally get to talk to somebody who knows how to help them, and they're very happy that I stop the horseshit, and stop asking about their childhood, and don't talk about the weather, etc. And I get *right away* to what bothers them. I tell them in 5 minutes. I've just explained to you the secret of most emotional disturbance. If you really followed what I said, and used it, you'd never be disturbed about practically anything for the rest of your life!

C-50: Uh-huh.

T-51: Because practically every time you're disturbed, you're changing *it would be better* to a *must*! That's all neurosis is! Very, very simple.

Now, why should I waste your time and not explain this—and talk about irrelevant things?

C-51: Because perhaps I would have followed your explanation a little better if I hadn't been so threatened initially.

T-52: But then, if I pat you on the head and hold back, etc., then you'll think for the rest of your life you have to be patted on the head! You're a bright woman!

C-52: All right—

T-53: That's another *should.* "He *should* pat me on the head and take it slowly—*then* a shit like me can understand! But if he goes *fast* and makes me *think,* oh my God I'll make an error—and that is awful!" More horse- shit! You don't have to believe that horseshit! You're perfectly able to follow what I say—if you stop worrying, "I *should* do perfectly well!" For that's what you're basically thinking, sitting there. Well, why *should* you do perfectly well? Suppose we had to go over it 20 times before you got it?

C-53: I don't *like* to appear stupid!

T-54: No. See. Now you're lying to yourself! Because again you said a sane thing—and then you added an insane thing. The sane thing was, "I don't like to appear stupid, because it's *better* to appear bright." But then you immediately jumped over to the insane thing: "And it's *awful* if I appear stupid—"

C-54: [Laughs appreciatively, almost joyfully]

T-55: "—I *should* appear bright!" You see?

C-55: [With conviction] Yes.

T-56: The same crap! It's always the same crap. Now if you would look at the crap—instead of "Oh, how stupid I am! He hates me! I think I'll kill myself!"—then you'd be on the road to getting better fairly quickly.

C-56: You've been listening! [Laughs]

T-57: Listening to what?

C-57: [Laughs] Those wild statements in my mind, like that, that I make.

T-58: That's right. Because I know that you would like to make those statements—because I have a good *theory*. And according to my theory, people wouldn't usually get upset *unless* they made those nutty statements to themselves.

C-58: I haven't the faintest idea why I've been so upset—

T-59: But you *do* have the faintest idea. I just told you.

C-59: All right, I know!

T-60: Why are you upset? Report it to me.

C-60: I'm upset because I know, I—the role that I envisioned myself being in when I walked in here and what I [laughs, almost joyously] and what I would do and should do—

T-61: Yeah?

C-61: And therefore you forced me to violate that. And I don't like it.

T-62: And isn't it *awful* that I didn't come out greatly? If I had violated that needed role *beautifully*, and I gave him the *right* answers immediately, and he beamed, and said, "Boy, what a bright woman, this!" then it would have been all right.

C-62: [Laughing good-humoredly] Certainly!

T-63: Horseshit! You would have been exactly as disturbed as you are now! It wouldn't have helped you a bit! In fact, you would have gotten nuttier! Because then you would have gone out of here with the same philosophy you came in here with: "That when I act well and people pat me on the head and say, 'What a great woman I am!' then everything is rosy!" It's a nutty philosophy! Because even if I loved you madly, the next person you talk to is likely to hate you. So I like brown eyes and he likes blue eyes or something else. So you're then dead! Because you really think: "I've got to be *accepted*! I've got to act intelligently!" Well, why?

C-63: [Very soberly and reflectively] True.

T-64: You see?

C-64: Yes.

T-65: Now, if you will learn that lesson, then you've had a very valuable session. Because you *don't* have to upset yourself. As I said before, if I thought you were the worst shit who ever existed, well that's my *opinion*. And I'm entitled to it. But does it make you a turd?

C-65: [Reflective silence]

T-66: *Does* it?

C-66: No.

T-67: *What* makes you a turd?

C-67: *Thinking* that you are.

T-68: That's right! Your *belief* that you are. That's the only thing that could ever do it. And you never have to believe that. See? You control your thinking. I control *my* thinking—*my* belief about you. But you don't have to be affected by that. You *always* control what you think. And you believe you don't. So let's get back to that depression. The depression, as I said before, stems from self-castigation. That's where it comes from. Now what are you castigating yourself for?

C-68: Because I can't live up to it—there's a basic conflict in what people appear to think I am and what I think I am.

T-69: Right.

C-69: And perhaps it's not fair to blame other people. Perhaps I thrust myself into a leader's role. But, anyway, my feeling right now is that all my life I've been forced to be something that I'm not, and the older I get, the more difficult this *facade*, huh, this *appearance*, uh—that the veneer is becoming thinner and thinner and thinner, and I just can't do it anymore.

T-70: Well, but really, yeah, I'm afraid you're a little wrong. Because oddly enough, almost the opposite is happening. You are thrust into this role. That's right: the role of something of a leader. Is that correct?

C-70: Yes.

T-71: And *they* think you're filling it.

C-71: Everyone usually does.

T-72: And it just so happens they're *right.*

C-72: But it's taking more and more out of me.

T-73: Because you're not doing something else. You see, you are fulfilling *their* expectations of you. Because, obviously, they wouldn't think you are a leader, they'd think you were nothing if you *were* acting like a nonleader. So you are fulfilling their expectations. But you're not fulfilling your own idealistic and impractical expectations of leadership.

C-73: [Verging on tears] No, I guess I'm not.

T-74: You see, that's the issue. So therefore you *are* doing OK by them—by your job. But you're not being an angel, you're not being *perfect*! And you *should* be, to be a real *leader.* And therefore you're a *sham*! You see? Now, if you give up those nutty expectations of yourself and go back to their expectations, you're in no trouble at all. Because obviously you're doing all right by them and *their* expectations.

C-74: Well, I haven't been. I had to, to give up one very successful situation. And, uh, when I left, they thought it was still successful. But I just couldn't go on—

T-75: "Because I must, I must *really* be a leader in *my* eyes, be pretty *perfect.*" You see, "If I satisfy the world, but I know I did badly, or less than I *should*, then I'm a slob! And they haven't found me out, so that makes me a *double* slob. Because I'm pretending to them to be a nonslob when I really am one!"

C-75: [Laughs in agreement, then grows sober] True.

T-76: But it's all your silly *expectations.* It's not *them.* And oddly enough, you are—even with your *handicap*, which is depression, self-deprecation, etc.—you're doing remarkably well. Imagine what you might do *without* this nutty handicap! You see, you're satisfying them while you're spending most of your time and energy flagellating yourself. Imagine what you might do *without* the self-flagellation! Can you see that?

C-76: [Stopped in her self-blaming tracks, at least temporarily convinced, speaks very meaningfully.] Yes.

One can see the active–directive nature of this session. From early on, Al used humor to encourage the client to feel more at ease and to reduce her fears (T-5) and at times expressed himself in an exaggerated and humorous manner (T-54) to elicit a more realistic and less horrified perspective (C-54, C-55). Throughout the session, he was consistently direct, honest, and straightforward (T-7) and exposed the client's exaggerations, irrational beliefs, and illogical jumps (T-6). He considered worst-case scenarios (T-9, T-15) and the ongoing tendency of the client to revert to *should* (T-16, T-29). Al gave realistic hope and optimism (T-10) that she could learn healthier ways. He invited her to focus in on main problems, kept presenting the rational perspective (T-28), and demonstrated healthy nondemanding language (T-29). He pointed out the difference between preferring and demanding (T-30, T-35) and between rational and irrational (T-54), and he pointed out the roots of Sara's emotional disturbance (T-40, T-51)—of her depression (T-12, T-16, T-68) and anxiety (T-49). More humor creates comfort and rapport (T-32). Al encouraged the client to focus on evaluating her thinking (T-14, T-56) and at various times assessed her grasp of the theory (T-35, T-60, T-67) and of how she created her disturbances. He continued to expose her demands and need for approval (T-53) and more of her irrational beliefs (T-63). He pointed out her unrealistic expectations of herself (T-73), her perfectionistic demands (T-75), and her self-flagellation (T-76). Clarification and encouragement were presented (T-76).

In one brief 15-minute session, Sara acquired awareness about what she did to create her disturbances and was given realistic hope that she could change her tendencies to do so. She was taught some of the main principles of REBT and how she could change her dysfunctional thoughts and feelings by disputing her irrational ideas and replacing them with rational philosophies.

Al was relentless in exposing the client's self-defeating ideas, boldly challenging them, educating her in the healthy approach, and expressing encouragement and belief in her capacity for changing her dysfunctional ways. He demonstrated unconditional acceptance of her, without accepting her harmful tendencies, and the difference is clear. Honesty and humor contributed to rapport. His ability to anticipate her views and beliefs, which he would then challenge, also contributed to rapport development in that it gave the client a sense of being understood. He didn't do all the "work"; he regularly asked questions that allowed Sara to think about what she was doing to contribute to her upsetness, and her answers indicated her grasp of what he was conveying to her. The philosophy and method of REBT were consistently conveyed to enable her to get a good grasp of them so that she would be able to apply them to future dysfunctional thinking and feeling and to behaviors she may experience and perform; hence her session attended to more than just the problems presented within it. With ongoing effort and application of what she learned, lasting change would be possible.

Depressive Disorders

Applying REBT's active–directive theory and practice to those who are severely depressed, and perhaps suicidal, is effective for a great many of them. Deeply depressed states, especially when the clients have endogenous depression (biochemically related), usually take much longer to change (A. Ellis, 1976, 2001b).

When a therapist first sees clients with depression, it is recommended to determine from what they present, and from their (and their family's) history, whether they are reacting mainly to adversities such as serious loss, trauma, or disability (reactive depression) or whether they suddenly "out of the blue" feel depressed, with a lack of energy or interest in life and activities, for no apparent reason. If the latter is the case, they may have endogenous depression. The therapist inquires about past and present medications for emotional and other problems. If it is suspected that they suffer from endogenous depression, more details are sought about their personal and family history, and the advisability of getting a psycho-pharmacological evaluation from a psychiatrist and of considering anti-depressants and any other appropriate medication is discussed. Many clients may resist medication, and if they do, I tell them during session that "we'll begin REBT by itself," which may work well if they *strongly* and *persistently* use it. If the client appears to be too disturbed to benefit from therapy alone, I later make it clear that medication in addition to therapy is most probably advisable. Nonfunctional and suicidal clients require psychiatric consultation and—for some—hospitalization.

Most frequently, whether the client is or is not on medication, I actively reveal the chosen and self-created irrational beliefs that probably largely instigated the reactive depression—absolutistic shoulds, musts, and other grandiose demands on self, others, and external conditions. I briefly explain the ABCs of emotional disturbing. I show how the client can independently recognize irrational beliefs, actively dispute self-depressing insistences, and considerably reduce them and change them to healthy preferences.

Clients suffering from depression frequently believe two very debilitating musts: First, "I must perform important tasks well and be approved by people I find important, or else I am an *inadequate, worthless person.*" This kind of self-downing is most common in depressed people. Second, "People and conditions I live with *absolutely must* treat me considerately and fairly, give me what I *really* want, and rarely seriously frustrate me! Or else, I *can't stand* it, my life is *awful*, and I can't enjoy it at all."

It is extremely rare to find clients with depressive tendencies and feelings who do not have these two main dysfunctional beliefs, or any of their innumerable variations. Even when they are endogenously depressed, their biochemistry encourages them to think crookedly, so that their interrelated thoughts, feelings, and behaviors are all involved in their moodiness.

In the first session or two, clients' irrational beliefs are identified, and I begin teaching them how to discover and dispute their self-sabotaging beliefs. We also explore the possibility of their depressing themselves about their depression, and if they have this secondary symptom, we show them first how to reduce their upsetness about the depression and then to reduce or eliminate the original depression. Many clients find it less difficult to remove the secondary symptom than the primary one. As with other disorders, clients with depressive ones are usually given a number of cognitive, emotive, and behavioral methods to help them minimize their disturbance and their disturbances about this disturbance. The methods chosen and tried depend on the unique qualities of each individual; REBT techniques will vary with each client.

The time taken to overcome depression depends on several important factors: first, on how depressed clients make themselves through their irrational convictions and for how long they have been disturbed; second, on whether their biochemistry is seriously unstable; and third, on the kind, degree, and persistence of the adversities in their lives.

Although clients may have relatively little choice about these factors, they have a great deal of choice about how they think, feel, and behave about the adversities that affect them. Humans are born and reared with opposing tendencies, such as the tendency to be disturbable as opposed to the tendency to change and correct self-defeating behaviors. With awareness, we have a choice about which of these tendencies we elect to use and whether we make ongoing efforts to change dysfunctional thinking, feeling, and behaving and the tendency to continue to make ourselves depressed and depressed about the depression.

An ultimate goal—REBT's elegant solution—would be to use REBT strongly and persistently to reduce feelings of depression and then to go on to make a profound philosophic–emotional change, in which one endorses one's healthy goals, desires, and preferences and minimizes absolutistic musts, shoulds, and demands. Self-downing, demanding, and awfulizing be gone!

Sandy was severely depressed because, at age 31, she had a double mastectomy and saw it as the most *awful* thing that had happened or ever could happen to her. She was sure that her husband, Tom, didn't love her anymore because he was disgusted with her body and no longer said what he had often said before, "I just love your breasts and can't get enough of them. How lucky I am!"

Sandy was also sure that if Tom ever left their marriage, her breastless condition would absolutely bar her from getting another "good man." She envisioned an endlessly lonely life and deemed that *awful*.

At first Al couldn't convince Sandy that losing her breasts was indeed very bad but not as bad as it could be and not *totally* bad. She could have died of breast cancer, he pointed out; further, she had several talents and pleasures, especially that of being a fine concert pianist and enjoying that pursuit. His anti-awfulizing fell on deaf ears. Because he was not a woman, she said, he just could not understand how *horrible* it was to be utterly breastless. Nor could he understand how *terrible* it would be for her to have breast implants, if her doctors thought that it was advisable. She kept her utterly rigid awfulizing! Besides, Tom would never be satisfied even if she had breast implants.

Getting nowhere at this stage with Sandy and her depression, Al tried again. He showed her that if she insisted on depressing herself about her double mastectomy, Tom would probably lose interest in her and in having sex with her *because* of her depression. Moreover, her refusal to try antidepressants was sensible because her depression was not endogenous but only followed after her loss of her breasts, and therefore antidepressants probably wouldn't work. To rid herself of her depression and save her marriage, she would have to accept herself fully with her disability. Nothing less!

Sandy finally got it—unconditional self-acceptance—indirectly, to save her marriage, instead of more directly, to save herself. She went over some of Al's books on acceptance, made self-acceptance her paramount occupation, and finally got it. Especially when she did poorly in her latest concert (mainly because of her depression), she thoroughly accepted herself with her mediocre performance and saw that she could do so. Then she included accepting herself with her flat chest. Finally, she saw that she could accept herself even if she lost Tom. Three crucial forms of self-acceptance! Sandy became regretful but not depressed, and she and Tom went on with their good life. Her next concert performance was one of the best she ever gave.

In a work currently unfinished in which I draw heavily on Al's work, I talk about using rational coping philosophies for overcoming depression, anxiety, and rage.[2] Here are some examples of rational coping philosophies that can, in addition to using other REBT techniques, help those who are depressing themselves about unfortunate events, if they repeat them to themselves often and forcefully:

- "It's bad, but it could be worse."
- "It's bad, but it could be much worse."
- "It's bad, but it's not awful."
- "It's bad, but I can still be happy in spite of it."
- "It's bad, but life goes on."
- "It's bad, but not that bad!"
- "It's bad, but I'm still alive and trying."
- "It's bad, but others are worse off than I am."
- "It's bad, but I can find some good in it."
- "It's bad, but I can learn some good things by experiencing it."
- "It's bad, but hassles like this can make me hardier."
- "It's bad to fail, but I succeed as well as fail."
- "It's bad, but it has a funny side that I can enjoy."
- "It's bad, but I can compromise and get some good from it."
- "It's bad, but I can still use it."
- "It's bad to be late, but better late than never."

Jessica had severe depressed moods because she had failed to finish college and constantly berated herself for quitting. When depressed, she promised herself to study hard on her own and get through correspondence school, and, after she read one of my books, she promised to reduce her self-berating. She did neither at first and more often fell into depressed moods. Al used several REBT methods with Jessica when he saw her for therapy, but the one that worked best was getting her to list all the disadvantages of her depression and to go over them 10 times a day while also listing all the disadvantages of her spending time, energy, and money therapeutically fighting against her self-damning and awfulizing.

---

[2]The author's website will include publication date and details on completion of the book at http://www.debbiejoffeellis.com.

As a result of doing this cost–benefit analysis, she strongly decided that the hassles of staying depressed were much worse than the difficulties of overcoming her awfulizing and self-damning. She gave herself a full year of applying several REBT methods no matter how difficult they were, and within 10 months she had her depressed moods down to occasional light ones. She almost slipped by rating herself as a "good person" for her therapeutic success instead of a person who had nicely succeeded. When she conquered this conditional self-esteem issue, she enjoyed her success with the cost–benefit analysis technique (which some other members of her therapy group were not succeeding at) without rating her *self* for succeeding.

One of Al's clients, Roderic, nicely used an example from one of Al's REBT books. The case Al presented was of a severely depressed man, Will, who had several years of ineffective therapy before his 12 sessions of REBT with Al. Will's first experience with REBT was when he volunteered to talk about his problems at Al's regular Friday Night Workshop in front of an audience of 150 people.

As was Al's custom, he showed Will during this public session how one of his main problems was lambasting himself for his procrastination at work and how he could, instead, give himself unconditional self-acceptance by damning his procrastinating but not himself. Will got this "revolutionary" idea immediately, especially when several people in the audience showed how they alleviated their depression by working at unconditional self-acceptance. Then Will saw Al for 12 sessions of REBT and solidly worked at achieving unconditional self-acceptance, especially with the use of REI. He went from being severely depressed—9 on a 10-point scale—to being moderately and occasionally depressed—2 on the same scale.

Roderic, whom Al saw for eight REBT sessions, told Al that he felt half-cured of his severe depression after reading Will's case in one of his books. Before Roderic saw Al, he used REI as Will had used it, and it helped him immensely. His eight sessions with Al also emphasized unconditional self-acceptance and anti-awfulizing, but although he never met Will and never attended Al's Friday night workshops (because he was an Orthodox

Jew who didn't travel on Fridays), he insisted that by modeling himself after the case of Will, he got off to a marvelous head start on his therapy.

Many other people have told me that by using a live model or using one from books (by Al and me or other writers), they have significantly helped themselves to overcome their emotional problems.

Julia, a 34-year-old with depression, at first seriously objected to Al's showing her that her conditional self-esteem for her intelligence and her writing accomplishments was greatly interfering with her truly achieving unconditional self-acceptance, but when he steadily showed her how harmful her self-protective excusing was and when he ruthlessly ripped up her harsh self-downing (mainly for her being depressed), she finally saw the light and was even more ruthless at attacking her conditional self-esteem. She apologized for her initial attacks on his directness and forcefulness and said that without it, she never would have broken through her perniciously praising her *self* instead of her good performances.

Al received numerous letters from former clients saying how they were practically horrified by his initial vigorous attacks on their crooked thinking–feeling–behaving. Eventually, sometimes years after he saw them for therapy, they got the reasons for his "attacks," began to distinctly rip up their own resistances, and greatly improved. Of course, he rarely heard from former clients who were still resisting his vigorously teaching them how to be vigorous. It would have been interesting to know whether they finally got it!

Al used REI with a suicidal man, Gregory, who had made one attempt to kill himself and end his depression, was on antidepressant medication, and still had suicidal moments. Al showed him that he was telling himself that life was hopeless, that he *must* not be a low-paid janitor, and that he was thoroughly worthless. If, Al said, he could accept himself with his disabilities, he would be much less depressed. Gregory said that this was probably correct, but he definitely could not accept himself as long as he had low-paid jobs, like his present one as a janitor; had subsistence pay; and was in debt. After seeing how adamant he was in clinging to his depressed state, Al gave him REI.

AE: Close your eyes, and think of one of the worst things that could happen to you: You only can keep your present job as a janitor; the tenants and the landlord keep yelling at you and telling you that you are no good; and your pay barely enables you to get by and pay your debts every month. Can you vividly imagine that happening?

Gregory: Imagine it? That's exactly the way it is. I'm several hundred dollars in debt. I barely could pay for my groceries this month.

AE: Good! Vividly keep imagining that things keep getting worse and worse.

Gregory: Oh, they do!

AE: Fine. You're really getting into this technique. Now how do you *feel* as you imagine the worst continuing to happen?

Gregory: Utterly miserable. Depressed. I'm thinking again of killing myself. [At this point, the audience members at my Friday night workshop began to show anxiety.]

AE: That's bad, but feel it as much as you can. Feel very down and depressed. Feel hopeless, hopeless. Really feel worthless and depressed. Feel it, feel it, let yourself really feel it.

Gregory: Oh, I do. Really do. I'm a hopeless mess. What's the use?

AE: You're really using this technique well! And in front of this audience, too. Again, feel very low and depressed.

Gregory: I couldn't feel worse.

AE: You're really cooperating! I like your guts! Feel very hopeless and depressed. Don't run away from it, don't repress it. And now, keeping the same negative image of your lousy position and your poverty, make yourself feel healthfully sorry and frustrated, very sorry and frustrated, but not, *not* depressed. You, like everyone, can control your feelings. So with the grim image that you are imagining, make yourself feel very sad and sorry but still not depressed.

The volunteer was silent, obviously struggling to change his feelings but not achieving it.

AE: OK, keep trying. It's hard, but you can do it. Make yourself *only* feel very sorry and frustrated, which are healthy feelings, rather than hopeless and depressed, which are unhealthy and which won't help you. You can do it, you can do it! Now tell me when you've done it.

Gregory: [After 2 more minutes of silence] I think so, I did it.

AE: Fine. *How* did you do it? What did you do to change your feeling?

Gregory: Well, I first said to myself, "Hell, it's been this way before, but it will probably change and get better as it did before."

AE: Yes? What else?

Gregory: Well, you gave me an idea when we were talking before. You said that I could accept myself with my disabilities, even with my depression. I could see myself as an OK person even when I was down and depressed.

AE: Why could you do that?

Gregory: Because, as you said, my worth to myself doesn't depend on my worth to other people.

AE: No, not if you don't *think* it does.

Gregory: No, not if I don't think it does. [At this point the members of the audience clapped vigorously.]

AE: Great. You really got it. But probably only lightly. You did remarkably well. But I want you to really solidly believe what you just said.

Gregory: Oh, I would like to.

AE: Fine. What I want you to do is this same kind of rational emotive imagery every day for the next 30 days. It only took a few minutes to do it this time. So do it every day for 30 days. First, imagine the worst—as you did. Let yourself feel very hopeless and depressed—as you again did. Then, with the same grim image, make yourself feel healthily sorry and frustrated, but *not* depressed.

Gregory: Sorry and frustrated, not depressed.

AE: Exactly. Once a day for 30 days in a row, until you train yourself—yes, train yourself—to feel sorry and frustrated instead of depressed, until after a while you will automatically and unconsciously feel that way. Are you willing to do this?

The volunteer agreed to do so. A few weeks later, I spoke to his psychiatrist, who said that he was significantly improved—sometimes still depressed but not suicidal.

REI does not always work. People do it lightly or for a few days and then stop. However, when they do it strongly and keep at it for even 10 or 20 days in a row, they often get good results, particularly in believing and feeling the philosophy of unconditional self-acceptance, as the volunteer, Gregory, seemed to do.

Extreme Anger

Once again, self-defeating demands abide at the heart of extreme anger and rage making, particularly the three main musts:

- "I absolutely must perform well, or I am an inadequate person."
- "You absolutely must treat me kindly and fairly, or else you are damnable."
- "Conditions under which I live absolutely must be comfortable, or else life is awful and I can't stand it."

Robert is a White man from a comfortable middle-class background; his family is Christian, although they rarely go to church. He considers himself "mostly atheist." As an adolescent, Robert was bigger than most other kids and prone to bullying them. He found that showing his rage to other youngsters was usually enough. Once they saw that he was really mad at them and observed his size, they allowed him to intimidate them without any fisticuffs. So he practiced showing his fangs and became adept at it.

As an adult of 28, Robert stopped most of his raging, but when it reoccurred, it absorbed him, distracted him, and hence kept him away from his studies of law; it also led many people to think him "crazy." He stopped most of his raging after some months of REBT. He succeeded at identifying his anger-creating demands with the help of his therapist and applied himself to vigorously disputing them and frequently repeating the rational preferences that replaced them.

Then, unfortunately, Robert, who was very handsome, stirred up prejudices of classmates by receiving the favor of women—both law students and teachers—and having affairs with them. He liked the sexual favors he received but hated his male and female jealous detractors and thought that they were prejudiced against him "for no good reason." He particularly hated two of his jealous female professors, who looked down on him for dating one of his other ex-professors. When the two jealous women gave him low marks, he went back to his old-time seething.

When Robert came to Al for therapy, he insisted that because his aptitude for law was just as good as it ever was, the two jealous professors "had no right whatever" in not fairly recognizing it and refusing to give him his well-deserved good marks. However, these two women perversely took the right that they supposedly didn't have and gave him mediocre marks. Robert raged on. Knowing how mad he was at them, the two professors appeared to go out of their way to zap him for this, he said. One of them gave his term paper a B grade when it was an A-standard paper. Robert felt furious.

Al helped Robert see that jealousy and unfairness were common conditions in human attitudes and behaviors and that his rage, if anything, was going to increase them, as it already had in the case of his two professors. Rage does not stop prejudice—quite the contrary!

At this point, Robert decided to change his tactics with the jealous professors. Although he strongly considered them unfair, he acted in nonhostile ways and even complimented them. He continued to do good work on his papers. Both of the professors started to give Robert the marks he "really deserved," and by the end of the term he got his A in both of their courses.

Better yet, Robert realized that his rage was crippling him and contributing to his obsessive ruminating about the professors' "perfidy." It was childish. So he went back to surrendering it, as he previously did when he achieved adulthood and stopped raging at his peers. He didn't quite achieve unconditional other-acceptance of the two professors, but he stopped ripping himself up about their perfidy.

Robert sincerely wanted to continue to stop his raging, having once moderated it but then having fallen back to its harmful habituation. He took the REBT steps of relapse prevention. He accomplished the following:

- He acknowledged that he was once again raging after temporarily giving it up.
- He assessed his rage as harmful to him and his relationships but didn't blame himself for feeling it. He criticized his raging but not himself. He didn't damn himself—only his behavior.
- He looked for his irrational beliefs that lay behind his rage. "They absolutely must not treat me unfairly." "Their unfairness is absolutely unforgivable!" "They are complete bastards!" "I can't stand their unfair treatment! I can think of nothing else!"
- He changed his godlike demands into realistic preferences. "They *do* have the right, as fallible humans, to treat me unfairly. Justice doesn't *have* to prevail!" "No matter how unfair they are, I can accept their behavior without completely condemning their personhood." "If I keep raging about their rotten behavior, I will obsessively keep it in mind. But I can stand it without liking it!"
- He disputed his irrational beliefs vigorously and persistently: "Unfortunately, they *must* treat me unfairly when they do!" "Their unfair *behavior* is wrong, but they also do some fair things and are not total bastards." "When I see that I *can* stand their rotten behavior, I will occupy myself with more pleasant things and stop obsessing about it."
- He looked for the many good things that he could find in life and purposefully pursued them to lead a useful, happier existence. He pursued friendships and associated with people who seemed to share his preferences and values, and he pursued hobbies and activities that he greatly enjoyed.

Low Frustration Tolerance

Low frustration tolerance (LFT) is a lack of acceptance of aspects of life that one does not prefer, like, or want. It contributes to the unhealthy emotional states of rage, self-pity, and depression.

It is not only those with problems of addiction and substance abuse who suffer from LFT. LFT can also be seen as a form of discomfort–anxietizing. Many people suffer with it. Typical irrational beliefs that contribute to creating their LFT are the following:

- "It's quite hard to quickly do this project I've accepted. It *should be* easier!"
- "It's not only hard to do this thing that I'd better do, it's *too* hard. I can't do it now!"
- "People absolutely must not act as frustratingly and badly as they do to me!"
- "I *can't stand* great or prolonged frustration!"
- "What is happening to me is *totally* bad—therefore it's *awful!*"
- "I can't do anything to cope with this horror, so I can't face it and deal with it!"
- "I *absolutely must* find something enjoyable to distract me from this terrible frustration!"
- "Even thinking about this horrible situation will completely upset me, so I won't think about it."
- "This frustration is *so* bad that I can't be happy *at all* if I attend to it!"

In doing REBT with clients who have serious discomfort–anxietizing or discomfort–depressing, the therapist can use many cognitive, emotive, and behavioral techniques (A. Ellis, 1979a, 1979b). It is particularly helpful to often show clients the cost–benefit ratio of their pleasurably indulging today—and their paying the grim price tomorrow. The therapist helps them make a long list of the pains of procrastinating and not doing what they "can't stand" to do, showing them that while it is quite hard to do onerous things today because they "can't stand" not doing so, it is much harder to do them later. Clients are also shown how to model themselves after people with great handicaps who nonetheless pushed themselves to be productive. Several REBT emotive techniques, such as REI, shame-attacking exercises, forceful coping statements, vigorous disputing, and role-playing, are also helpful.

Behaviorally, the REBT therapist helps clients with discomfort–anxietizing (and with other anxietizing) to stay in difficult situations and work on their LFT until it is lessened, to reinforce themselves when they promptly do difficult tasks they are avoiding, to sometimes penalize themselves when they cop out of doing them, and to use additional REBT behavioral methods.

The ultimate goal for the REBT therapist and client is to strive to achieve the "elegant" REBT solutions to LFT and to

- minimize the clients' most destructive aspects of their discomfort–anxietizing,
- look for and reduce any of its other aspects that they may not talk about at first,
- try to help them rarely resort to serious LFT,
- encourage them to use REBT methods constructively if they relapse and do afflict themselves with LFT again,
- push them to commit themselves to working against their potential LFT for the rest of their lives, and
- unconditionally accept themselves if they keep only mildly disturbing themselves when faced with unusual frustrations and restrictions that may occur and if they relapse.

Perfectionism

This self-defeating way of being has at its heart the irrational beliefs of people who believe they should always be competent, achieving, and adequate in every way if they are to be considered worthwhile; that it is awful, terrible, and catastrophic when things aren't the way they want them to be; and that there is a right, precise, and perfect solution to problems, and it is catastrophic if the perfect solution is not found.

It can be seen as a form of obsessive–compulsive disorder.

It is rational to want self-efficacy and good solutions to problems, but escalating the "want" to a "must," as the perfectionist does, leads to anxiety, depression, and other unhealthy negative emotions. Often they will create secondary symptoms—for example, thinking it is "awful" and "imperfect" to feel anxiety will lead to anxiety about the anxiety.

Perfectionists tend to be highly conditional self-acceptors who base their worth as persons on achieving perfectly and also on doing better than others.

Perfectionists are more rigid and dogmatic in their irrational beliefs than are many nonperfectionists.

The REBT therapist will work with clients to help them understand that demanding, rather than preferring, perfectionism will create anxiety, depression, self- and other-damning, and LFT and often gets them less of what they want. Many of the cognitive behavioral and emotive REBT techniques, such as vigorous disputing of the musts, risk taking, daring intentionally to act imperfectly to see whether the world indeed comes to an end, and shame-attacking exercises, can help to change their demands to preferences.

Addiction and Personality Disorders

Not all addicts are alike. Many factors contribute to people's addictiveness. Although some clients are "nice neurotics"[3] with LFT who want (demand) what they want when they want (demand) it, a large percentage also have severe personality disorders (PDs). People with PDs may be more prone to addiction. Many clients have multiple addictions (dual diagnoses; Penn & Brooks, 2000; Velten & Penn, 2010).

It is important for therapists to recognize the differences between "nice neurotics" with addictions and people with severe PDs and to use the appropriate REBT cognitive, emotive, and behavioral methods described in this book. Most important is teaching such clients to have unconditional self-acceptance, unconditional other-acceptance, and HFT.

---

[3]In his witty and compassionate manner, Al used this term with the intention of encouraging people with neuroses to adopt a humorous acknowledgment and acceptance of their self-defeating tendencies, which, with effort, they had the power to change.

Before I describe REBT application to clients with addictive behaviors, I have a few words about those with PDs: Clients with some kind of PD often appear to be, in *Diagnostic and Statistical Manual of Mental Disorders* (fifth ed.; *DSM–5*; American Psychiatric Association, 2013) terms, paranoid, schizoid, antisocial, borderline, avoidant, dependent, and/or obsessive–compulsive. When they are not quite diagnosable in these PD categories and are labeled *neurotic*, they are seen to be prone to endogenous anxiety, panic, depression, and rage with innate, biological tendencies to overreact easily, underreact to the stresses and strains of everyday living, or both.

Many individuals with severe PDs come from homes in which family members also were innately highly disturbable. Therefore, their childhood as well as adulthood involved more stressors than many others tend to experience. Thus, the interaction between their innate disturbability and their poor environment contributes significantly to making them even more upsettable than they otherwise would have been. However, people who are biologically easily disturbed will often think, feel, and act in self-defeating ways no matter how favorable their early and later environments are.

People with severe PDs tend to start off with several main elements of disturbance: First, they have strong biological tendencies to think, feel, and behave destructively, especially in complex social relationships. Second, they have poor life consequences (C) that they therefore create and are inflicted with because of their biological and social handicaps. Third, the interactions among their poor adversities (As), dysfunctional beliefs (Bs), and self-defeating consequences (Cs) take a toll.

Because of their innate—and environmentally exacerbated— deficiencies, they may have unusual difficulties with all the ABCs of human disturbance. At point A (adversity), they have more unfortunate experiences than do nonhandicapped children (e.g., they may have more disturbed parents who may criticize or overprotect them because of their peculiarities). At point B (belief system), they think crookedly about their unusual As (because of their innate and acquired cognitive–emotive deficiencies) and therefore end up with severe PDs.

People with severe PDs may be more prone to addiction than are "nice neurotics" when they have more As and disturbed Cs, and they then make themselves more frustrated than those without such handicaps. Because of greater and often overwhelming frustrations, many develop unusual degrees of LFT, and because of their greater failures and rejections, many of them also develop neurotic self-damnation about their deficits, handicaps, and failings. Some, for biological reasons, may be more prone to *demand* that they must not be frustrated and must perform well and may be more prone to demanding. Thus, for both biological and environmental reasons, persons with PDs often feel so disturbed that they feel compulsively driven to alcohol, drugs, smoking, food, gambling, and other addictions to allay their disordered thoughts, feelings, and actions temporarily. Those with obsessive–compulsive disorder (OCD) and other PDs may have neurological anomalies that interfere with normal appetite- and desire-controlling brain centers and that decrease their ability to stop their compulsive indulgences.

A basic REBT approach for those with addiction and relapse issues—both with and without PDs (A. Ellis & Velten, 1992)—is for the therapist to attend to the following:

- Help clients identify the irrational beliefs they tell themselves before indulging or relapsing and to forcefully dispute these beliefs.
- Help clients identify any self-damning and realize that the more self-damning, the more they may want to indulge in their addiction for the purpose of avoiding it.
- Help clients unconditionally accept themselves, while not accepting their destructive behavior—that is, to blame the foolish acts but not themselves, their essence, or their personhood.
- Continue to teach and reinforce that although clients' acts may be foolish and self-destructive and they are responsible for them, nonetheless, they as people are always acceptable, worthy, and able to work on changing destructive ways.
- As clients are succeeding in staying off their addictions, assign various REBT exercises to challenge any self-downing and to help the client

to act against depression and anxiety. These exercises include shame-attacking, REI, writing cost–benefit ratio lists for resuming the destructive using and addictive behavior versus staying off it, ongoing forceful disputing of irrational beliefs, and more.

- If clients have relapsed or are procrastinating and not doing homework assignments, encourage them to continue to work against any self-downing and also to identify any rationalizing or denials about the relapse or procrastination and show that these may make them feel OK in the short term but in reality prevent recovery and improvements of behavior, thoughts, and feelings. REBT teaches clients to have unconditional self-acceptance, to acknowledge mistakes, and to work at correcting them. The less self-damning, the better the progress.

- If clients have LFT about their emotional disturbances (such as thinking they can't stand feeling anxious or depressed), help them understand their LFT and urge them to face it, without awfulizing it, so they are less likely return to the addictive substance or behavior to escape the pain of the anxiety or depression. The REBT therapist helps them accept that they can stand their anxiety or depression, and while they are "standing" it, they can work on reducing it. Running away or numbing themselves will in all probability make the disturbing emotions worse. Clients can be encouraged to see that with ongoing application of REBT methods, they can temporarily live with their disturbances as they make efforts to change them into healthy and appropriate emotions (e.g., concern, disappointment).

- Pursue ongoing application of REBT, with the aid of an appropriate support group, to help clients become steadily and increasingly less easily disturbed and decrease the chance of relapse to addiction.

Borderline Personality Disorder

Individuals with borderline personality disorder (BPD) seem to be born with innate emotional difficulties, such as being dysthymic, depressive, easily enraged and panicked, histrionic, and high-strung. They often exhibit behavioral difficulties such as hyperactivity, hypervigilance, and impulsivity. They may be obstreperous, interruptive, excessively restless, temper ridden, and antisocial and often are alienated, addictive, over-dependent, inattentive, and purposeless (Cloninger, 2000). Often they exhibit cognitive difficulties such as attention–deficit disorder, rigid ways of thinking, inability to organize well, impulsive thinking, forgetfulness, inconsistent images of others, inability to maintain a sense of time as an ongoing process, learning disability, perceptual disability, proneness to be double-bound, a tendency to exaggerate the significance of things, rigidity, demandingness, severe self-downing, purposelessness, impairment in recalling and recognition, and deficient semantic coding. Individuals without BPD may have these organic cognitive deficiencies, but they usually have them less intensively, cope with them better, and exhibit them largely under stressful environmental conditions, whereas individuals with BPD tend to have them more endogenously and more severely (Cloninger, 2000; Linehan, 1993).

The main characteristics of BPD include a pattern of unstable relationships, self-damaging impulsiveness, affective instability, intense inappropriate anger, recurrent suicidal threats, marked and persistent identity disturbance, chronic feelings of emptiness or boredom, and frantic efforts to avoid real or imagined abandonment (American Psychiatric Association, 2013).

According to REBT theory, individuals with BPD tend to observe or sense their deficiencies and put themselves down for having them. They often demand that they *must* not act inadequately, berate themselves for acting that way, and easily feel like inadequate people, which individuals with BPD often tend to feel anyway and which will then be significantly exacerbated.

They tend to be jealous and hostile toward less dysfunctional people, will insist that these individuals *must* not have greater advantages than they have, and will often show, as *DSM–5* notes, "inappropriate, intense anger or difficulty controlling anger (e.g., frequent displays of temper, constant anger, recurrent physical fights)" (American Psychiatric Association, 2013, p. 663).

They tend to create or exacerbate their natural LFT by demanding, "I must not be as handicapped by and looked down upon for these handicaps as I indubitably am!" Thus, they will easily have and aggravate, as *DSM–5* observes, "identity disturbance: markedly and persistently unstable self-image or sense of self" and "frantic efforts to avoid real or imagined abandonment" (American Psychiatric Association, 2013, p. 663). If and when they observe their borderline characteristics and the real handicaps they bear in society, they often once again tend to demand neurotically that (a) "I must do better than I am actually doing!" (b) "Other people absolutely must not treat me unfairly for my handicaps!" and (c) "The conditions under which I live must not be so handicapping! It's awful and I can't stand it when they are!" When they act in these ways, individuals with BPD make themselves more disturbed—and more borderline. Moreover, they usually then tend to take their hatred of themselves, of others, and of their handicaps into their therapy, upset themselves about it and about their therapists, and again make their condition and their potential for improvement much worse.

Because of their innate cognitive, emotive, and behavioral impairments and because of self-downing and LFT about these impairments, individuals with BPD become even more dysfunctional. Their self-deprecating and discomfort intolerance about their impairment tends to make them still more impaired, still more disturbed about their dysfunctions, and then still more impaired. A vicious cycle ensues, in the course of which impairment encourages disturbance, disturbance promotes more impairment, and greater impairment encourages more disturbance.

This vicious circle can be partially alleviated using REBT if individuals with BPD are helped to minimize their self-denigrating and their LFT. However, their original cognitive, emotional, and behavioral deficits, which often present them with tendencies to hold on to musturbatory, rigid demands that lead to self-downing and intolerance of frustration, block them from alleviating their dysfunctioning and often seriously exacerbate it.

As is done with every client, REBT therapists do their best to effect the greatest possible improvement for their BPD clients but realistically expect limited gains with most of them, because many may be more resistant to change than are other clients and may not make consistent or sufficient effort to effect change because of their LFT, short-range hedonism, and attentional and focusing deficiencies. The therapist is recommended to work on having unconditional other-acceptance, HFT, and patience when working with clients with BPD.

REBT with a BPD client usually includes the following:

- Revealing and disputing their irrational and self-defeating thoughts. Their perverse ways of thinking may be self-serving—for example, they may attempt or threaten suicide to control others and induce them to give in to their way to satisfy their need for attention or to make some other point. Several techniques may work to make disputing effective, including the dialectical or oppositional persuasive techniques of Marcia Linehan (1993), Benjamin's (1996) method of using the client as a consultant, or the paradoxical and metaphorical method that Hayes (Hayes, Strosahl, & Wilson, 1999) used with agoraphobic patients (but that can also sometimes be used with BPD). Because clients with BPD are often clever in holding on to their disturbances, the therapist who is equally clever at disputing sometimes wins out. Although clever and well-calculated therapist ripostes sometimes win the game, sticking to the strategy of regular REBT therapy with its cognitive methods is probably more effective in the long run.

- Teaching clients with BPD specifically how to unconditionally accept themselves and that they can choose to rate only their thoughts, feelings, and behaviors, not themselves, their total being, or their essence. They can acknowledge their BPD handicap but not damn themselves for having it.

- Showing clients with BPD the self-defeating effect of LFT and how to ameliorate it, particularly by strongly disputing the demands inherent in it. The goal is achieving HFT.

- Encouraging clients to achieve unconditional other-acceptance.

- Discussing the fact that some medications taken by clients with BPD, including antidepressants, have bad side effects, and some do not work for this population. The REBT work of helping clients increase their frustration tolerance and decrease their resistance to medication to avoid the unpleasant side effects can help them be willing to keep trying to get the most appropriate medication and to tolerate its side effects.

As psychopharmacology evolves, perhaps its advances, along with those in psychotherapy, may combine to better cure people with BPD of more of their extreme and difficult borderline states. However, even at present, the efforts by clients with BPD and therapists, although difficult, can bring improvements and be rewarding.

Obsessive–Compulsive Disorder

In a later section of this chapter, I describe the case of Arthur, a client with OCD, and provide additional explanations, so this section is brief.

As with clients with BPDs, important goals in REBT therapy for clients with OCD are the following:

- working hard to achieve HFT;
- developing unconditional self-acceptance, unconditional other-acceptance, and unconditional life acceptance;
- using a number of REBT methods—cognitive, emotive, and behavioral—such as
    - disputing irrational beliefs, realistically, logically, and pragmatically;
    - doing cost–benefit analysis;
    - using rational coping statements;
    - sharing REBT with others;
    - modeling;
    - doing homework—writing down their ABCDEs;
    - using psychoeducational materials;
    - using forceful coping statements—forcefully;
    - using rational emotive imagery;

- doing shame-attacking exercises;
- audio-recording forceful disputing;
- role-playing and reverse role-playing;
- using in vivo desensitization;
- remaining in "bad" situations while increasing their HFT; and
- using reinforcements and penalties.

For some people with OCD, it is hoped that, in addition to REBT sessions, they see a good psychopharmacologist and take appropriate and effective medication as required.

Posttraumatic Stress Disorder

A main cause of posttraumatic stress disorder (PTSD) is that people who suffer traumatic shock awfulize greatly about it, which can result in their suppressing or repressing it. Not facing the trauma and not working through it makes it likely that feelings about the trauma will continue to be felt and continue to arise.

The REBT therapist will work with clients who have PTSD to reveal and dispute core musturbatory philosophies and demands. Imaginal exposure, REI, and risk taking with some real exposure to desensitize from the shock can be of effective help. Being alert to secondary symptoms—such as panic about panic—is important, after which work is done to reduce or remove it. Clients are shown that their cognitions, which may have served them as useful defenses at the time of the trauma, are now affecting their lives negatively (Paulson & Krippner, 2007).

Several REBT methods—cognitive, emotive, and behavioral—can help significantly, in addition to the ones mentioned earlier, including the vigorous disputing of beliefs that the trauma should not have happened, that the client should have prevented it, or that not preventing it makes the sufferer a worthless and inadequate person. When a client believes that recovery is impossible, the REBT therapist is encouraging about the possibility of healing and change that comes from steady application of the methods, and the therapist can recount examples of others who have suffered traumas but went on to get better and live good lives.

Psychoeducation about the PTSD condition and its consequences is helpful. Learning that severe recurring reactions and other symptoms they had suffered were expectable and common can help reduce awfulizing.

After a session, or sessions, with the therapist empathically listening to the client and normalizing the panic reactions, the client is often then more able to discuss REBT theory and practice and be more receptive to REBT, as applied to their PTSD condition.

It is important that the client work on acquiring unconditional self-acceptance. The therapist continues to show unconditional other-acceptance for the client. Doing cost–benefit analysis on avoidant behavior, among other things, can be helpful as a prelude to in vivo exposure work. At times, skill training is helpful and encouraged— for example, assertiveness training for clients who have become overly withdrawn.

Many of the individual and group therapy clients that Al and I worked with had trouble dealing with the brutal and tragic events of September 11, 2011. Some of those who witnessed the events firsthand developed PTSD. It was clear to us, though, that if enraged American and worldwide citizens kept their irrational beliefs, such as damning oneself for feeling powerless, damning the terrorists for what they did, and damning the world for being so cruel, they would continue to enrage themselves against the terrorists and their backers and likely encourage them to increase their fury against Americans and other people who oppose them. Likewise, this would encourage more retaliation by terrorists, returned by Americans again, and so on. History has amply shown that love begets love and that hatred and violence beget increased hatred and violence.

Whenever Al was asked how REBT could help people cope with the tragic events of September 11, he responded in the following way:

First, you can use REBT to teach yourself—and others—unconditional self-acceptance. With unconditional self-acceptance, you fully accept yourself with all of your warts and flaws, while heartily disliking and doing your best to change some of your self-defeating and antisocial behaviors.

Second, you can use REBT to unconditionally accept all people as fallible humans, no matter how badly they act. You can firmly try to induce them to change their self-sabotaging and immoral thoughts, feelings, and actions. However, you work hardest to unconditionally accept the sinners, but not their sins.

Third, you unconditionally accept life, with its immense problems and difficulties, and teach yourself to have high frustration tolerance. As theologian Reinhold Niebuhr said, you strive to change the unfortunate things that you can change, accept—but not like—those that you cannot change, and have the wisdom to know the difference.

If you achieve a good measure of these three REBT philosophies—that is, unconditional self-acceptance, unconditional other-acceptance, and unconditional life-acceptance—will you therefore convince terrorists to change their absolutistic, bigoted ways? Not exactly. However, you will cope much better with terrorism, help others to cope with it, and model behavior that can, if you strongly encourage it to be followed by more people around the world, eventually reduce it. This will take many years to effect and will require immense and persistent educational efforts by you and your supporters to promote peaceful and cooperative instead of hateful and wavering solutions to serious national and international difficulties. However, not working, in your own head and in collaboration with many other human heads, to produce this long-term purpose will only ensure renewed terrorism for decades, and perhaps centuries, to come. Are you willing to keep relentlessly working for REBT's recommendations of self-peace, peace to other humans, and peace to the world? If so, you may help people of good will to think, plan, and produce eventual answers to terrorism and to many other serious world problems.

Family, Marriage, and Relationship Issues

Individuals within any relationship can create their own emotional–behavioral disturbances from the beliefs they construct about those with whom they relate. REBT reminds people that only they can change their irrational beliefs; they cannot make others change, and effective REBT therapy includes teaching them how to choose to respond to others and possibly change important aspects of the system. It points out that where there are problems, the client in all likelihood has dysfunctional thinking, feeling, and behaving that significantly interrelate with the dysfunctioning of the other(s). In REBT partnership, marriage, and family therapy, these interconnections and how they may be corrected are discussed. The therapist will focus on the following:

- helping the individuals acquire unconditional self-acceptance (A. Ellis, 2005b) whether or not they are receiving adequate love and attention from the others involved, and even if they are failing at fulfilling any or all of their responsibilities within the partnership or family;
- helping the individuals achieve unconditional other-acceptance (A. Ellis, 2005b), thereby fully accepting the others even when they are behaving badly or neglectfully (this does not mean accepting bad behavior but remembering and accepting the fallibility of every human being); and
- fostering HFT so that the individuals involved can endure, and even at times enjoy, some of the challenges of relationships.

The REBT cognitive, emotive, and behavioral methods already described in this book are applied. The therapist teaches the appropriate methods to the clients, who can reinforce what they are taught in an ongoing manner, by attending REBT workshops, lectures, and seminars; reading books; listening to CDs; watching video recordings on REBT; and attending weekly REBT group therapy.

REBT can be effectively used with children and adolescents (A. Ellis & Bernard, 2006), and they benefit most when their parents are also using and applying it to themselves—in other words, when the parents are modeling the healthy behaviors and attitudes that they would like their offspring to learn and practice in their daily lives. I have used, demonstrated, and taught many of my clients to use it successfully, as did Al as well as Albert Bandura (1997) and other psychologists (A. Ellis, 2005b). Our years of practice showed Al and me that "do-as-I-healthily-do" behavior demonstrated by parents, along with appropriate reinforcement and penalizing, is more authentic, and can be more successful, than an authoritarian "do-as-I-say, not-as-I-do" approach when teaching their children.

REBT is considered one of the approaches in psychology and psychotherapy that most encourages self-sufficiency and the self-empowerment of clients through its teaching of tools and techniques (A. Ellis, 2010). Effective REBT therapists do their best to motivate their clients to rely increasingly on their knowledge of, and most especially their application and practice of, REBT. With time, practice, and perseverance, the healthy beliefs and attitudes become a habitual part of the client's experiences.

I work alone now, without my husband, since his death in July 2007. I often share with clients and the people I teach in presentations and workshops how I have used, and continue to use, the principles of REBT. They have helped me continue to live a productive life, despite the intensely difficult challenges of the final years of my husband's life and the pain and grief of living without him since then. I am living proof of how well REBT works when it is vigorously applied.

Older Clients

The elderly population is growing, and those older clients with emotional disturbances are well served to receive good therapy that is particularly mindful of the added factors they endure.

In addition to their human proclivity for self-disturbance, many older clients have health difficulties and frailties, which contribute to emotional vulnerabilities. As many of them survive the deaths of relatives and friends, their support groups decrease at the same time that they are experiencing grief from losses, changes in work, entry into retirement, financial concerns, or moving and domestic challenges. They may feel less effective, more restricted, and bored. If, as younger adults, they did not learn how to deal with or change negative painful emotions, it is much harder for them to cope with these factors. Some may feel increasing hopelessness and futility about life.

As with clients of all ages, the REBT therapist expresses empathy for the clients and their unique-to-them issues and problems. The therapist offers realistic hope and focuses on possibilities for life enhancement while not denying or dismissing the difficult aspects that cannot be changed. The therapist pays attention to particular physical disabilities the client may have and responds kindly and accordingly. For example, if the client has poor hearing, the therapist will raise the volume of his or her voice and talk clearly and at a good pace.

Various irrational beliefs are common to many older clients, including the following:

Self-Downing Irrational Beliefs

- "I must do as well as I previously did when I was younger and more able, or else I am an inadequate person."
- "I should look younger and more attractive than I am."
- "I must not be physically weak and deficient."
- "I should have accomplished more than I did during my life."
- "I must not look as anxious and weak as I now do."
- "I must not die and be forgotten."

Anger-Creating Irrational Beliefs

- "Other people must treat me kindly and fairly, especially because of my age and the limitations and disabilities that go with it. When they treat me shabbily, they are rotten people."
- "My relatives and friends must not neglect me and must treat me as well or better than they did when I was younger."
- "Other people should treat me as well as they did when I was younger and more able."
- "People should not discriminate against me or look down on me because of my age and my weaknesses."
- "Relatives and friends should remember all the sacrifices I made for them, be grateful, and treat me in a special way."

LFT Irrational Beliefs

- "The conditions of my life must be as good as they previously were, and it's *awful* and *I can't stand* it when they aren't."

- "The special problems and difficulties of old age should not exist and it's *too hard* to live with them."
- "I *need* more pleasure, freedom from restrictive conditions, and excitement, and life is too boring without it."
- "I *need* more companionship and love, especially from those I care for."
- "I should be able to do the work I used to do to fill my life and make it more interesting."
- "I should have the health I used to have and not be ill or disabled."
- "I should not have to be as dependent on others as I now am."
- "I should not have to die and be deprived of life."
- "I shouldn't be going through what I am going through."

REBT therapists and clients work together to help clients accept the reality of deprivation, change, and aging while changing what they can to enhance their lives, even with their limitations. Together they use REBT empirically to dispute dysfunctional and irrational beliefs, asking where the evidence is that older people must do as well as they did when they were younger and more able. They use REBT logically to question whether the clients will *always* perform poorly and will be *inadequate people* if they sometimes or often do. They use REBT pragmatically to encourage clients to ask themselves what results they will achieve if they demand that they absolutely must do as well as they did when younger and if they believe they are worthless individuals if they do not function as well as they did in their youth. They form, and vigorously use, rational coping statements such as the following:

- "As bad as it is, it could always be worse."
- "I can be grateful for the good in my life."
- "I can still enjoy my life despite my restrictions and handicaps."

The therapist helps clients model themselves after others they know, or know of, who overcame their limitations. Al's book *Rational Emotive Behavior Therapy: It Works for Me, It Can Work for You* (A. Ellis, 2004) can be helpful in this regard. He wrote it months after life-saving surgery in his 90th year. It includes sections by both Al and me on how Al coped and provides recommendations of actions and attitudes that can be helpful to apply before and as we age. Additional psychoeducational materials may be recommended to elderly clients that can motivate and inspire them to cope better and improve their attitudes.

REBT therapists help clients to reframe some of their hassles. They teach relaxation and other helpful distraction techniques and encourage their clients to involve themselves in absorbing interests and to stay active. They emphasize problem solving and provide information about services older clients can use to compensate for any absence of familial or social support. They teach the clients unconditional self-acceptance and continue to demonstrate unconditional other-acceptance.

True to its multimodal approach, REBT emphasizes whichever of its additional methods seems most appropriate for the individual elderly client, such as shame-attacking exercises, REI, appropriate risk taking and in vivo desensitization assignments, use of reinforcement and penalties when applying new risk-taking activities and exercises, skill trainings, and developing HFT.

Encouraging and facilitating opportunities for the elderly to help or contribute in some ways to other people and causes can also be healthy activities and involvements for them, which can bring rich and added meaning to their lives.

Morbid Jealousy

To conclude this chapter, I look briefly at the application of the REBT approach to morbid jealousy but remind readers that additional destructive emotions and conditions that have not been referred to specifically here can also be significantly helped with the use of the REBT approach, as can be seen from the previous sections of this chapter that addressed diverse conditions.

Irrational or morbid jealousy consists largely of demanding, rather than rationally wanting and preferring, a level of attention, love, and devotion from others. Yet again, REBT therapists encourage clients to identify and change absolutistic musts and perfectionistic demands into realistic and rational preferences. Some of the main antijealousy techniques are disputing irrational beliefs; using rational coping statements, forcefully; reframing (looking at the situation as a challenge for growth rather than a catastrophic horror); cost–benefit ratio; cognitive distraction; REI; achieving unconditional self- and other-acceptance; role-playing; use of humor to keep a healthy perspective; reinforcement methods; and healthy risk taking. These techniques were described in Chapter 3 of this book.

EXAMPLE OF USING LONG-TERM REBT WITH A CLIENT

Arthur, a White American man in his 40s and a highly talented musician, was a client whom Al treated individually for more than 7 years; 2 years into individual therapy, Arthur also started attending group therapy led by Al and me. I continued to provide individual therapy to Arthur after my husband's passing.

Arthur had OCD, along with occasional panic attacks, depression, and other conditions. He would often partake in massive binge eating. In addition to receiving REBT, he was seeing a psychiatrist and taking a medication.

Arthur would wash his hands over and over whenever he would suspect they were "contaminated" with any germs or dirt. This might take place 50 or more times a day. He would repetitively check to see that his oven was turned off and that gas wasn't leaking out of it. Before his performances, he would go through a specific ritual in which he would tap his piano a set number of times. He believed that if he didn't do this, his performance would be no good. Great amounts of time and energy were being wasted on these rituals. He would feel panic if he thought he had not tapped the correct number of times, followed by panic about the panic and its disabling effect on his piano playing. Because of his OCD and other tendencies, he also suffered from huge self-downing. He would damn himself for his disabilities, saying he was weird, warped, and ugly. He was not obese but somewhat overweight (probably in large part due to his eating binges and lack of exercise), and his skin looked pasty and pale. He was sure no woman would ever like him, so he avoided social contact with them and remained lonely and without relationships. In reality, although a little plump, he was not unattractive to many, and sometimes women would approach him after his jazz performances. Nonetheless, he felt painfully shy, would make little eye contact, and missed probable opportunities to make future dates with some of these women.

OCD takes many forms and seems rarely to be about one thing. It usually begins in childhood or adolescence and may last a lifetime. It may also accompany serious neurological disorders, including Huntington's disease, Sydenham's chorea, Pick's disease, postencephalitic parkinsonism, and Tourette syndrome.

Neuroimaging studies tend to show that dysfunction of the frontal lobes of the brain and the frontal-caudate circuit are associated with idiopathic OCD. Successful treatment of OCD with clomipramine (Anafranil), fluoxetine (Prozac), and other serotonin agents tends to show that deficiencies in the neurotransmitter serotonin are often involved with OCD (American Psychiatric Association, 2007).

Cognitive distortions, irrational demands, and the need for certainty may well be factors in creating OCD, but it is not clear whether biological deficiencies create this "need" or whether they block individuals with OCD from interrupting and giving up this "need" when they see that it is doing them harm. Quite likely, both of these issues are involved.

People with OCD, including practically all whom Al and I saw over the years, also frequently have other related personality disorders, such as severe panic states and serious depressive disorders. They may also be addicted to alcohol, drugs, nicotine, overeating, or gambling. Some of these afflictions may be reactions to the difficulties that ensue from their obsessive–compulsive behavior (as seemed to be the case with Arthur), but some of these afflictions may be affected by biological and neurochemical factors.

The REBT theory of causation of severe personality disorders, including OCD, holds that affected individuals usually have cognitive, emotive, and behavioral deficits and that they then have irrational beliefs or cognitive distortions about having these deficits and the difficulties of living that accompany them (A. Ellis, 2001b). Thus, cognitively, those with OCD probably have more aspects of learning disability and focusing (or overfocusing) handicaps than do what I call "nice neurotics." Emotively, they tend to be overactive. Behaviorally, they are prone to disorganization, procrastination, and compulsivity. Such deficits, again, can partly be reactions to their OCD. However, it is highly likely that these are also, at least in part, biological deficiencies.

As I have discussed, cognitive distortions, or what are often called irrational beliefs, seem to be part of the human condition. People with neuroses have them fairly frequently, and virtually all humans make themselves somewhat neurotic. Those with OCD, like other people with personality disorders or psychoses, not only have the usual kinds of irrational beliefs, but they may (again, for biological reasons) hold them more rigidly and strongly than "nice neurotics" do.

Moreover, because neurotic cognitive distortions are about life's adversities and handicaps (e.g., "I hate failing and therefore I must not fail!") and because OCD itself is a handicap, people with obsessive–compulsive personalities usually make themselves neurotic about their disorder, and their neurosis consequently aggravates their OCD and their other life problems.

In Al's 50-plus years of working with clients with OCD, he found that a number of REBT methods, particularly in vivo desensitization or exposure and activity homework assignments, usually worked to cut down tedious ruminating and gripping compulsions—when clients consistently and steadily used them.

Reality Check and Symptom Description

Al had Arthur list his compulsions and symptoms, their severity, and their frequency. He also listed situations in which, or after which, he frequently felt panic, overate, acted impulsively, and performed rituals. He listed the repetitious thoughts, feelings, and urges that led to his panic, along with their severity and the intensity of their disturbance. He listed the consequences he feared would take place if he stopped his rituals.

Action

For homework and in our sessions, having learned the ABC method, including the modes of disputing irrational ideas, Arthur would dispute the irrational beliefs that led to his panic and to the anxiety that preceded the rituals. His homework was to write the ABCs of his situation each day, along with the disputation and effective new philosophies. Al and he would also use the ABC method to remove his secondary symptoms (of panic about the panic and anxiety about his anxiety). When he revealed in some sessions that he had not done the homework that had been assigned to him in the previous session, Al and Arthur would explore the reasons, identify the irrational beliefs involved, and dispute them.

Some of these irrational beliefs were the following: "It's too hard and I can't stand doing this homework; I will never be able to change." "I shouldn't have to keep doing this homework." "It shouldn't be this hard." "If I can't see great results by now, it proves I am hopeless and doomed to suffer from my condition forever, so why bother?"

After disputing these beliefs and coming up with healthy and realistic beliefs and attitudes, Arthur usually felt remotivated and did better at completing his homework in the period that followed.

When he did not do his homework and felt he was relapsing, Al reminded him that relapse is common. The important thing was to accept that fact, accept himself with his human tendency to relapse, and pick up and make an effort again.

Another homework exercise was to write cost–benefit analyses of continuing the rituals versus stopping them. It was clear that the benefits of stopping outweighed the short-term benefit of relief when not stopping them.

He was directed to schedule obsessive behaviors and rituals at specific times only, for only limited periods, and to think about and perform his other daily activities at other times. Over time, Arthur was encouraged to lessen his assigned time for the rituals, which he succeeded in doing with increasingly few relapses. He kept on hand a list he had written of distraction activities he could do to interrupt or postpone his OCD behaviors, such as vigorously repeating healthy coping statements, writing music or words in his journal, playing around on his piano (imperfectly and spontaneously, as opposed to seriously rehearsing), reading, yoga, meditation, breathing techniques, and so forth.

Arthur was encouraged to do what he was afraid of to lessen and, over time, eliminate his fears. In relation to his shyness, he was given the homework assignment of saying hello to a stranger every other day and, after some weeks of success with this, to do it more often and to gradually and consciously make more eye contact when he did so.

After many months of this homework, Arthur was also given the task of speaking with women who approached him after his shows, even for only a few minutes, instead of avoiding them. Over time, as his shyness decreased, he allowed himself at various times to invite a few of the women he felt comfortable with for coffee or some other sort of date. One such date with a woman led to an enjoyable longer period of ongoing dating and friendship.

His willingness to join group therapy after a couple of years of individual therapy (which continued) also forced him to confront his shyness and to interact with others. This proved to be beneficial with regard to overcoming his shyness and other issues. With regard to his binge eating, he was encouraged to throw out most of the unhealthy junk food he had in the house and to have healthier food in the house to replace it.

The various REBT methods and activities we applied were spread out over time, and specific issues were attended to as they came up. Arthur worked steadily at them for the most part, and he frequently used certain applications of REBT methods, such as disputing, to achieve unconditional self-acceptance, especially when he slacked off.

Unfortunately, many people with OCD do not do such steady and persistent work. Many find it extremely difficult to cut back on their dysfunctional behaviors, and if they do, they easily return to their former habits or create a set of new ones. The lack of organization in the lives of some, along with their time-consuming obsessions, contributes to their not following, or only partially following, the cognitive, emotive, and behavioral methods of REBT. A number of clients with OCD, however, do significantly improve with effort and succeed in reducing their obsessive–compulsive behaviors and thinking by using REBT methods regularly, along with appropriate medication.

Arthur did manage to change significantly and to perform fewer rituals, overcome much of his shyness, generally avoid secondary symptoms (panic about panic) and—importantly—develop unconditional self-acceptance of himself with his disabling tendencies. Progress took time, however, and there were many periods when he slacked off, did not do the homework, and indulged in harmful habits and rituals before he would push harder to resume applying the REBT methods. When Arthur lapsed, Al would make sure he was frustrated not with Arthur but only with his *behaviors.* It was important that Al modeled and demonstrated unconditional other-acceptance with him. Arthur's involvement in both individual and group therapy was of great benefit to him. Individual therapy gave Al more time to focus on his issues than was possible in group therapy, and group therapy gave Arthur some additional time to work on his issues, with group members contributing their ideas, support, and reinforcement to him. In return, Arthur had the opportunity to listen to others' problems and contribute his suggestions and support to them.

What else was done to contribute to Arthur's improvements?

- Psychoeducation: Arthur was taught the principles of REBT in sessions and encouraged to attend Friday night workshops, general REBT workshops, and lectures. It was recommended that he read certain books, including *The Myth of Self-Esteem* (A. Ellis, 2005b); *Feeling Better, Getting Better, Staying Better* (A. Ellis, 2001a); and *A Guide to Rational Living* (A. Ellis & Harper, 1961, 1975, 1997).
- Al also discussed OCD to give him a more concrete and objective understanding of the condition. One of Arthur's homework assignments was to research it further.
- He was told that there was definitely hope that he could improve the quality of his life and reduce the OCD if he persistently, consistently, and forcefully made an effort and was committed to such improvement.
- He was reminded that his OCD could have a strong biological or innate tendency that made change difficult and that he may not completely overcome the condition, but with ongoing effort, he could minimize it.
- He was reminded that no matter how well or poorly he did, he was still a worthwhile human being, just because he was alive and kicking! His tendencies might not be OK, but he was.

OBSTACLES OR PROBLEMS
IN USING THE REBT APPROACH

Although I believe (possibly with some subjective bias!) that REBT is one of the best and most effective approaches for most people with disturbances much of the time, and research certainly supports REBT's efficacy, it does not help all people all of the time (just as any one therapy does not). A number of things contribute to lack of success, obstacles, and problems using REBT.

For example, humans are born with biological tendencies, later augmented by environmental and cultural factors in their upbringing, to think crookedly and irrationally, and resistance to new ideas and approaches is an outcome of this. Also, some clients who have previously had psychoanalysis or other forms of therapy than REBT may resist the active–directive nature of REBT. Such clients may want to go on and on about their past, as they are used to doing in therapy, and may balk at the REBT therapist's attempt to bring their focus more to the here and now, to taking greater responsibility for identifying their part in creating their present emotional disturbances, and to what they can do to undisturb themselves.

Clients with learning difficulties who do not understand the principles and methods of REBT cannot be expected to apply them, or even to apply some of them. Individuals who have severe biological disturbance and imbalance, mania, delusions, autism, or any of the various psychoses, who are out of contact with reality, or who are otherwise mentally disabled are normally not helped with REBT alone and usually require concurrent medical treatment. Custodial or institutional care is required for some of them. Some individuals suffering psychoses may experience comfort and contact with reality when on appropriate medication and can experience benefit from applying REBT in addition to taking the medication. Rather than either–or, I recommend both–and in such instances.

As previously indicated, REBT is more effective with clients who have a single major symptom and with clients of average and above-average intelligence. Clients with greater severity of symptoms (e.g., severely depressed) may tend to make less effort to change the faulty thinking that contributes to their emotional state. Persistence, patience, and vigorous reminders from the therapists about the benefits of the clients making strong efforts, along with reminders about the detriments of not doing so, can help to motivate some of these clients. Clients with serious disturbances are more innately predisposed to faulty and rigid thinking, and this lack of flexibility will hinder or prevent healthy change. Clients who are strongly inhibited or defensive may be unaware of some of their underlying problems and, more often than not, do not allow themselves to feel. Although REBT is successful with such clients at times, at other times its active–directive approach may not succeed in pushing them out of their inertia so that they finally acknowledge and work on their issues and problems.

Individuals who expect magical cures and easy improvements are less likely to make the effort required for substantial change; unmotivated and unresponsive clients (who may have felt "forced" to come for therapy for reasons such as their parents or partners pressuring them to do so or those who are in therapy for court-mandated reasons) frequently avoid participating in the homework and actions that can help them. Fortunately, when therapists persist with vigor and encouragement in helping them, some of these clients drop some, or much, of their resistance.

Individuals with LFT, who want, or demand, instant gratification and who are unwilling to delay short-term gratification for the good of long-term gratification and well-being, often will not make the effort that could provide healthy changes. They may be unwilling to do REBT homework and put forth the required effort. Clients with rigid agendas and who are not interested in making changes within themselves to create healthy, instead of unhealthy, emotions by learning to think and act in rational ways and who simply want the therapist to fix their problems (e.g., wanting the therapist to help them make a partner who left them for another person come back to them) will rarely be receptive to guidance regarding self-work and self-responsibility. Individuals with traits such as grandiosity or narcissism of large measure are less likely to be receptive to any honest feedback about their self-defeating ways, especially if the feedback contradicts what they believe.

Lack of focus and commitment, forgetfulness, and unsustained effort on the part of clients limit their potential for healthy growth and change.

Physical illness, sleep deprivation, grief following loss, malnourishment, and exhaustion make it harder for individuals to focus and act on changing dysfunctional thoughts, emotions, and actions. By the same token, therapists who act in un-REBT-like ways with the client or who are poor at performing their role may hinder a client's potential progress (e.g., if the therapist has LFT for the pace of the client's progress and expresses it through lack of unconditional other-acceptance, impatience, or criticizing the client, as opposed to criticizing deficient behavior). Other factors that can affect the outcome of therapy include a therapist who is, or appears, distracted during sessions and somehow conveys a lack of genuine interest in helping the client or one who allows or—worse—encourages clients' neediness for approval or who conveys that he or she needs approval from the client. Therapists who talk too much, do not listen enough, or do not adjust their manner according to the individual before them also have less successful outcomes. Therapists behaving in any of these ways can learn to unconditionally accept themselves with their flaws but not accept their harmful behavior— and preferably will push themselves to change their unhelpful ways.

It is important for REBT therapists to think carefully and choose wisely the REBT methods they practice with, and recommend to, their clients. With one client, for example, REI didn't work, and after observing that, I suggested she no longer use REI. Meredith was a client with BPD who made herself angry at practically everyone in her life—her parents (who actually were outstandingly patient, loving, and supportive of her), her boss, and often President Bush. In the REI exercise, she imagined feeling furious at her parents for buying her a birthday present she hated. Instead of doing the next step of the exercise, which invited her to change her fury to healthy negative emotions of sadness or regret or frustration, she escalated her anger—and kept herself angry at her parents for the next 2 months!

REI—great method! Meredith—wrong client for it!

To conclude this chapter, I remind readers that REBT can be applied, with great success, to a variety of clients with a variety of disturbances, issues, and conditions. The therapist's skill, attentiveness, and appropriate application of REBT can enhance the process, and I hope that therapists not only practice it with clients but also use REBT on themselves.

5

Evaluation

Rational emotive behavioral therapy (REBT) is the pioneering cognitive behavior therapy (CBT) of the 20th century. Recent meta-analysis demonstrated its effectiveness currently and over the past decades regardless of clinical status, age of sample, and delivery format; however, David, Cotet, Matu, Mogoase, and Stefan (2018) asserted that more studies need to be conducted, along with more psychometrically sound instruments to uniformly measure REBT mechanisms of change. However, it appears that few of the outcome studies on the method have been of the caliber of those on cognitive therapy (A. T. Beck, Rush, Shaw, & Emery, 1979) and on CBT (Barlow, Esler, & Vitali, 1998; Meichenbaum, 1977). Some of the reasons during Albert Ellis's lifetime include the following: The Albert Ellis Institute had been primarily a training institute for therapists and not an academic research institute. Most students had been focused on developing their clinical expertise and building their

http://dx.doi.org/10.1037/0000134-005
Rational Emotive Behavior Therapy, Second Edition, by A. Ellis and D. Joffe Ellis
Copyright © 2019 by the American Psychological Association. All rights reserved.

practices, with secondary interest in research, and because the institute awarded certificates, not degrees, to graduating fellows, it had been unable to motivate most to do the thorough research they would do for a master's in psychology or social work or a doctorate. Also, the cost of good research studies is high, and it had been too expensive for the institute to sponsor them. Some staff members who committed to doing extensive research failed to follow through. Another reason is that the theory of REBT is applied to most, rather than to distinct, disturbances. Published studies have usually focused on particular aspects of disturbance, such as depression, anxiety, or anger, so the fact that the same underlying philosophy applies to a number of disturbances may have led to fewer studies using REBT for specific disturbances. Another aspect of REBT that may have discouraged research is its favoring the use of a large number of cognitive, emotive, and behavioral techniques such as those described in previous chapters of this book. This approach differs from the fewer cognitive and behavioral methods used in other cognitive behavioral systems. Therefore, it is difficult to test the relative effectiveness of the various techniques used in REBT.

In addition to the study mentioned above, REBT found support in the comprehensive survey of meta-analyses that offer empirical validation for CBT in various clinical applications by Butler, Chapman, Forman, and Beck (2006). Butler et al. showed CBT to be most efficacious in unipolar depression, generalized anxiety disorder, panic disorder with or without agoraphobia, social phobia, posttraumatic stress disorder, and childhood depressive and anxiety disorders.

Hundreds of research studies have validated the major theoretical hypotheses of REBT (A. Ellis & Whiteley, 1979). Furthermore, because many REBT techniques are found within CBT, it also has validation through CBT's substantial research. In particular, the research of Aaron T. Beck and his associates supports the clinical hypotheses of REBT (Alford & Beck, 1997). More than 1,000 other studies have shown that the irrationality scales derived from the Ellis list of irrational beliefs correlate significantly with the diagnostic disorders with which these scales have been tested (Hollon & Beck, 1994; Woods, 1992). REBT, the pioneering CBT, and Beck's CBT significantly overlap with early cognitive-therapy approaches of Janet (1898), Dubois (1907), and Adler (1929), as well as with existential–humanistic and behavioral therapy. REBT is also exceptionally eclectic and integrative, as is Arnold Lazarus's (1989) multimodal therapy. Together, CBT and REBT have been tested in more than 2,000 outcome studies, the great majority of which have shown them to be more effective than other forms of therapy and that when clients are shown their irrational and dysfunctional beliefs and taught the methods to change them, they tend to become less neurotic and less afflicted with severe personality disorders (Hollon & Beck, 1994; Lyons & Woods, 1991; McGovern & Silverman, 1984; Meichenbaum, 1977; Silverman, McCarthy, & McGovern, 1992). REBT uses a much more philosophical approach than do the other schools of CBT, referring to this as the *elegant approach*, which focuses on changing a person's underlying philosophy of life and demands rather than symptoms alone. Meta-analyses by Engels, Garnefski, and Diekstra (1993) and Lyons and Woods (1991) have evaluated its efficacy. Blau, Fuller, and Vaccaro (2006) found a strong relationship between REBT's main philosophical disputes and the comprehensive personality model of Costa and McCrae (1992a, 1992b).

REBT has been found effective for depression (David, Szentagotai, Lupu, & Cosman, 2008), side effects of breast cancer treatment (Montgomery et al., 2014; Schnur et al., 2009), psychotic symptoms (Meaden, Keen, Aston, Barton, & Bucci, 2013), parental distress (Joyce, 1995), and disruptive behavior (Gaviţa, David, Bujoreanu, Tiba, & Ionuţiu, 2012).

REBT in conjunction with medication has been found to be more effective than medication alone for major depression (Macaskill & Macaskill, 1996). The same has been found for dysthymic disorder (Wang, Jia, Fang, Zhu, & Huang, 1999). REBT has been shown to be an effective adjunctive treatment with inpatients with schizophrenia (Shelley, Battaglia, Lucely, Ellis, & Opler, 2001). It has also been shown superior to control conditions in the treatment of obsessive–compulsive disorder, social phobia, and social anxiety (Dryden & David, 2008). Studies demonstrate its efficacy for obsessive–compulsive disorder (Emmelkamp & Beens, 1991) and social phobia (Mersch, Emmelkamp, Bögels, & van der Sleen, 1989). REBT and CBT have been investigated and found effective in family relationship therapy in a number of research studies, summarized by Baucom and Epstein (1990); A. T. Beck (1988); Hayes, Jacobson, Follette, and Dougher (1994); and Jacobson (1992). A unique study by Faucher and Kiely (1955) showed that the REBT philosophy is especially useful in the treatment of elderly individuals.

In 15 articles in the January 2000 special issue of *American Psychologist* on positive psychology, edited by Martin Seligman and Mihaly Csikszentmihalyi (2000), many outstanding psychologists and researchers reviewed studies to show which factors likely contribute significantly to positive psychology and the minimizing of cognitive–emotional–behavioral dysfunctioning. Al and I were pleased to discover that these authorities on the psychology of human happiness largely agreed with REBT's main therapeutic ideas about self-disturbance.

No research has yet been published on the basic tenet in REBT: that people largely disturb themselves by thinking in terms of absolutistic shoulds and musts. I fervently hope that such studies will be performed—solidly and soon. I hope that more outcome research will be done, especially in specific areas such as anxiety, depression, anger, addiction, and relationship issues. I hope that the relative effectiveness of core REBT procedures versus those of general CBT and other therapeutic systems will be investigated. I hope that several main cognitive, emotive, and behavioral techniques will be tested to see whether they support each other—as I hypothesize they do—or whether some of them are relatively ineffective. I encourage research to be done on the effectiveness of REBT as a self-help approach.

It is ironic that because of the immense popularity of Al's many self-help books over the past 50 years—thanks in part to therapists recommending them to clients—they have been wrongly seen as light and superficial and that as a result some academics and "scientific" professionals may have held prejudiced views of his work and discouraged research on it. Alfred Adler (1931), who wrote many of his main books for the general public instead of the profession, was similarly neglected.

When a great deal more research is conducted to investigate the effectiveness of REBT, I am confident that it will continue to validate what Al and I clinically observed in our work—the effectiveness, elegance, and efficacy of REBT.

SPECIFIC PROBLEMS AND CLIENT POPULATIONS FOR WHICH REBT IS AND IS NOT EFFECTIVE

As noted earlier in this volume, REBT is most effective when used with bright individuals who are motivated to change, who are willing to embrace REBT's humanistic and life-enhancing philosophy, and who make the ongoing effort required for solid and lasting change.

It is not usually effective with individuals who have severe learning difficulties; who have strong psychoses that render them out of touch with reality; who exhibit resistance, laziness, low frustration tolerance, and the desire for change to be easy and effortless (i.e., magical thinking); and who have narcissistic, rigidly dogmatic, and hypomanic tendencies.

HOW DOES REBT WORK WITH DIVERSE CLIENTS?

REBT has achieved good results with individuals from diverse cultures and religions (Nielsen, Johnson, & Ellis, 2001) and with schoolchildren (Seligman, Revich, Jaycox, & Gillham, 1995). It pays attention to the mores, language, and taboos that clients of foreign cultures and diverse religions express and believe and, as far as possible, will support clients' life-enhancing goals—and help them achieve them—within the context of their culture and religion, without trying to change these facets of their lives.

A good many clients from diverse cultural backgrounds who have been helped with REBT have been victims of prejudice, and some have suffered persecution from biased and bigoted people around them. As a result, some made themselves depressed and felt hopeless, whereas others enraged themselves about the injustice in the world and the dastardly behavior of their persecutors. REBT encourages such clients to accept the reality that life is often unfair, to change what they can—if anything—to realize that their depression or rage was not helping the situation but hurting them, to identify the specific irrational beliefs creating their debilitating emotions, and to dispute those beliefs vigorously and often. Ongoing effort is required, particularly to achieve good measures of unconditional self-acceptance, unconditional other-acceptance, and unconditional life-acceptance.

When using REBT with clients of different cultural backgrounds, the skillful therapist will usually adapt his or her manner, voice, and language to that with which the client is most comfortable, when appropriate. It is helpful for the therapist to relate examples to the client, when possible, that are understood in the culture of the client. It is important, especially when the client's first language differs from that of the therapist, that the therapist check the client's grasp of what is being discussed if he or she is in any doubt; patience and longer explanations of REBT concepts may be required.

REBT recommends that the effective therapist is respectful of a client's religious or cultural beliefs and practices cultural humility (Johnson, 2016a, 2016b), courtesy, and what Johnson called "ethical REBT" (Johnson, 2001)—reminding us of how important it is that attention be given to the unique ethical concerns that arise when REBT practitioners treat devoutly religious clients or clients presenting with uniquely religious problems. It is vital not to ignore clients' religious variables altogether and to be mindful about thoughts of directly challenging and disputing specific religious beliefs that clients hold. Studies have shown the efficiency of REBT with religious clients (Johnson, 2008; Nielsen, Johnson, & Ridley, 2000). Practitioners are strongly encouraged to reflect on and examine their own religious beliefs and beliefs about other religions and to educate themselves about aspects of religion that pertain to their clients. Johnson, Ridley, and Nielsen (2000) described categories of religious sensitivity and proposed a framework for religiously sensitive psychotherapy to consider when practicing REBT.

Because of the essential commonsense, humanistic, and down-to-earth nature of REBT, it has much in common with aspects of the philosophies of many societies and cultures and therefore may be comfortably understood and applied. In many societies and cultures, REBT concepts (e.g., self-interest, social interest, tolerance, self-acceptance, other-acceptance, life-acceptance, acceptance of ambiguity, acceptance of reality, commitment, healthy risk taking, rationality, flexibility, scientific thinking) are understood. In our years of clinical experience, Al and I observed the efficacy of REBT with clients from diverse backgrounds when properly understood and applied.

CONCLUSION

I strongly and enthusiastically invite readers who are in the research field to investigate the areas suggested earlier in this chapter to add to the research done thus far and to conduct more studies that demonstrate and validate the immense efficacy and effectiveness of the REBT approach that Al and I, and countless other practitioners and clients, observed and experienced over the years.

6

Future Developments

I believe that the future of psychology and psychotherapy will be highly integrative but will largely and significantly consist of the theory and practice used in rational emotive behavior therapy (REBT) and cognitive behavior therapy (CBT).

Since Al's passing, it appears that many writers and presenters have not been giving REBT its due credit as being the original form of CBT. Some practitioners and former REBT teachers who had studied REBT with Al are now combining it with CBT and consequently are neglecting to incorporate or emphasize some of the unique features of REBT in their work. Such practitioners have started to call it "rational emotive and cognitive behavior therapy" with the intention of arguing that REBT simply has a role in the larger CBT paradigm (David, Cotet, Matu, Mogoase, & Stefan, 2018). This is a misrepresentation of REBT's contribution to the psychotherapy field, and the combining of the two approaches in that way

http://dx.doi.org/10.1037/0000134-006
Rational Emotive Behavior Therapy, Second Edition, by A. Ellis and D. Joffe Ellis

was not the desire of its founder, Albert Ellis. He and I had substantial discussions about this issue. We concluded that REBT is both at the heart of, and unique from, the CBT umbrella. Not only did REBT herald the cognitive revolution in psychotherapy, it also offers stronger emphases that are not included in other cognitive approaches, including elements such as unconditional acceptance, attending to one's essential life philosophy, vigor and precision in disputing irrational beliefs, striving for elegant solutions to issues concerning one's mental and emotional well-being, and exercising gratitude and mindfulness as daily practices.

An additional observation of interest is that as time goes on, some distinct aspects of the REBT approach have been taken, renamed, somewhat modified, and presented as new approaches in psychotherapy, with no credit given to the shoulders on which they largely stand.

It has also been apparent that some students in recent years have the false impression that REBT was developed *after* CBT. Aaron T. Beck himself acknowledged the influence of Albert Ellis and REBT on the formation of his cognitive therapy work, which was presented in the 1960s, over a decade after REBT's emergence (A. Ellis, 2010; A. Ellis & Harper, 1961).

It is my hope that students and practitioners can become aware of the accurate facts in the history and development of psychology and psychotherapy and the vital role played by REBT.

To make clear to current and future theorists, students, and practitioners the unique and distinct qualities of REBT and to prevent hybridization, teachers of psychology, counseling, comparative psychotherapies, and related subjects need to be responsible in teaching accurate accounts of the history, development, and current status of the various approaches in our field and point out clearly the similarities and differences between REBT and CBT. The American Psychological Association Theories of Psychotherapy series, of which this book is a part, offers concise yet substantial descriptions of the main psychotherapeutic approaches, as do a good number of textbooks that are regularly revised and updated on those topics.

Both REBT and CBT attend marvelously to the cognitive and behavioral side of humans; however, REBT from its beginnings equally attended to the importance of understanding emotions. Al clarified the difference between unhealthy and healthy negative emotions. REBT encourages an emotional life that is at times healthfully intense and enthralling, not a neutral one, to replace the debilitating unhealthy emotions described earlier in this book. REBT emphasizes the importance of incorporating attitudes of unconditional acceptance into our lives, along with gratitude and mindfulness.

It is my hope that a striking development in REBT will be that of a greater number of educators, theorists, and practitioners understanding the distinctions in the offerings of REBT and CBT, respectively, and that they will utilize each approach effectively as they deem most appropriate.

I believe that in addition to its ongoing effectiveness in individual and group therapy, REBT will increasingly be presented through psychoeducation and mass media, through which it has already informed inestimable millions of people over the past 6 decades. Workshops, lectures, and seminars will continue. Interviews and presentations through webcasts, podcasts, radio, and television will continue to inform people about the relevance and application of REBT in every aspect of their lives, as will REBT literature, CDs, and DVDs. Through its self-help materials, REBT can greatly help members of the public who do not elect to go to therapy. Self-help groups using REBT principles already exist and will increase. SMART Recovery (self-management and recovery training) for addictions conducts regular meetings throughout the United States in which REBT is followed and taught; this method continues to grow in popularity. Stress management training incorporating REBT in the workplace, in organizations, and in clinics is also popular, and I believe it will continue to be.

One of my greatest wishes is that REBT can be taught through regular schooling at every level—from preschool through high school, college, and graduate school. The value of young people acquiring emotional education, particularly in this day and age, is enormous. This has begun in some schools and colleges and continuing education programs. May it flourish and grow! The future of psychology and psychotherapy may well lie in the development and spreading of better methods of emotional education—specifically of rational emotive education or, as it is increasingly referred to now, rational emotive behavior education (REBE). Presentations on REBE have been given in Australia by Giulio Bortolozzo and me, and many more will be given by me and others in the United States and other countries. Bullying in schools appears to be an ever-present problem that REBT can help to reduce, as teachers and parents can use it with both the bullies and the bullied. Research on this has been done by Giulio Bortolozzo and Ken Rigby in South Australia (Rigby & Bortolozzo, 2013).

I continue to encourage therapists who favor approaches other than REBT to add aspects of REBT to their work. Many non-REBT therapists have written to me and Al over past decades expressing their appreciation of how some REBT cognitive, emotive, or behavioral techniques enhanced their work with their clients. At the North American Society of Adlerian Psychology annual convention, Al presented on REBT in past decades, and since his passing I have presented on it each year. Many of the attendees have reported believing that specific REBT techniques would be most compatible with their clinical approaches, and they enthusiastically shared their intentions to use them.

For years, REBT has reminded people of the destructive effect on our physical health when we experience and harbor unhealthy emotions such as rage, depression, and anxiety. For the past 4 or more decades, there has been increasing interest, based on research from both traditional and alternative medical fields, in the mind–body connection, and it continues strongly in the present day. The contribution of REBT as an effective tool for creating and maintaining a healthy mind, healthy emotions, and greater physical health and well-being in individuals is immense. I hope that research will be done to demonstrate that which I have experienced and witnessed time and time again: the life- and health-enhancing results in individuals who practice REBT.

REBT has been, and continues to be, presented to business groups; at "salons" that encourage dialogue about contemporary issues and perspectives, such as the International Center for Integrative Studies, at religious forums, and at other such public gatherings. As already mentioned, REBT can benefit all in society; as much as it is useful to health professionals, health practitioners, and their clients, I hope that, now and in the future, it is increasingly presented to varied public groups and gatherings for the benefit of all attendees.

Sadly, we live in a time of war, and many participants and survivors suffer from posttraumatic stress disorder (PTSD). Al wrote about the application of REBT to those suffering from PTSD (A. Ellis, 2001b). Service members and their families could be greatly helped by learning and using REBT. Paulson and Krippner (2007) have also written on this, and others have written that cognitive behavior approaches are the most effective treatments for PTSD (Friedman, 1994).

In a *National Psychologist* article (Gill, 2010), it was first reported that the U.S. Army was planning to require that its soldiers take training in positive psychology and emotional resiliency, and this has since been implemented. REBT principles, such as encouragement to adopt healthy thinking and attitudes, have been incorporated in these trainings. I hope that regular follow-up takes place to check on the progress (or lack thereof) of the individuals participating and that the partners and families of the soldiers are also offered such support and help.

I believe that when REBT is thoroughly practiced and presented, more people will steadily get better—not merely feel better. Hence, more clients will have reduced their disturbed feelings and behaviors and replaced them with healthy ones and will have profoundly changed their underlying dysfunctional philosophies into rational and compassionate ones. Increased practice and presentation and accurate education in comparative psychotherapeutic approaches, combined with more solid outcome studies, will reduce the marginalization of REBT and contribute to its further growth and popularity.

When this happens, REBT may well revolutionize psychotherapy in the 21st century, as it first did in the 20th century.

7

Summary

R ational emotive behavior therapy (REBT) has changed an enormous number of lives for the better, and, in all probability, it will
increasingly continue to do so.

REBT was the pioneering cognitive therapy from which, starting
a decade after it was originated, came other forms of cognitive therapy
and cognitive behavior therapy that incorporated its main methods. These
include George Kelly's (1955) pioneering personal construct therapy,
Aaron Beck's (1976) cognitive therapy, Maxie C. Maultsby's (1984) rational behavior therapy, William Glasser's (1965) reality therapy, Arnold
Lazarus's (1989) multimodal therapy, Donald Meichenbaum's (1977)
cognitive behavior modification, and Michael Mahoney's (1991) cognitive
therapy. In the acceptance and commitment therapy of Stephen Hayes
(Hayes, Strosahl, & Wilson, 1999), significant aspects of unconditional
self-acceptance, unconditional other-acceptance, and unconditional

http://dx.doi.org/10.1037/0000134-007
Rational Emotive Behavior Therapy, Second Edition, by A. Ellis and D. Joffe Ellis

life-acceptance are endorsed. REBT was incorporated into many self-help books and approaches and into both credible and cultish "self-awareness" groups and approaches of the 1960s to the present. Its benefits are felt by those who practice it—who take action when they recognize they are behaving, thinking, and feeling in self-defeating ways. People are introduced to the principles and practices of REBT through their individual therapy, group therapy, trainings, workshops, lectures, presentations, school and college courses, seminars, support groups, books, CDs, DVDs, articles in the press, interviews and stories on radio and TV, and word of mouth by others who use and benefit from it. I present REBT to both professional groups and members of the general public in the United States and in countries around the world.

REBT appeals to many because it is effective in creating healthy changes for people who apply it, is not complex or complicated, is practical and easy to learn for many motivated individuals, and does not foster (and in fact actively discourages when necessary) clients' dependence on the therapist or REBT teacher. In that way, it empowers its users, reminding them that *they* are responsible for their actions, thoughts, and feelings—that *they* control their emotional destinies.

It stands apart from most of the other cognitive therapies with its philosophical emphasis—particularly on the importance of unconditional self-acceptance, unconditional other-acceptance, and unconditional life-acceptance and the vigor and emphasis it puts on disputing the musts and shoulds. It is both pragmatic and compassionate by nature: both-and, not either-or. It is a holistic approach. It encompasses the vision that the more individuals make themselves healthy emotionally, mentally, and behaviorally, the more societies, cultures, and countries can benefit. Ultimately, this could reduce and prevent violence and terrorism. Ultimately, this could prevent the manifestation of the negative potential that humanity has to destroy itself through power mongering, wars, murders, and the neglect and abuse of other life forms and the natural environment in which we live.

REBT includes a number of main principles. It asserts that humans are influenced by both their biology and their environment and that we are born and reared with the capacity to think both crookedly and sanely. With awareness—thinking about our thinking—we have a choice about the ways in which we think, feel, and behave, and our emotions and behaviors result largely from the ways in which we think about, or perceive, ourselves, others, and the world around us.

When we think in rational and realistic ways, we create healthy and appropriate emotions and behave accordingly. When we think in irrational, rigid, and demanding (musturbatory) ways, we create unhealthy negative emotional and behavioral consequences. By disputing irrational beliefs realistically, logically, and pragmatically, we create rational beliefs and effective new philosophies to replace them and consequently feel and act in healthy and productive ways.

REBT constantly reminds us that to maintain a healthy and life-enhancing way of thinking, feeling, and behaving, ongoing and persistent work and effort are required. Cognitive, emotive, and behavioral homework assignments are given and followed up in the therapeutic setting, and people who are not in therapy can also give themselves such assignments. The assignments frequently include doing the ABCs of REBT, in written form, identifying the specifics of each of its following aspects:

A = Activating event,
B = Beliefs or belief systems (IBs = irrational beliefs; RBs = rational beliefs), and
C = Consequences (emotional, behavioral), and then vigorously
D = Disputing the IBs and coming up with
E = Effective new philosophies.

Further appropriate REBT techniques that can be applied include acknowledging and remedying any secondary symptoms; doing cost–benefit ratio assessments; using distraction methods, such as yoga, meditation, and breathing exercises; using modeling methods; using educative and reinforcing materials such as books (bibliotherapy), CDs, and DVDs; using the rational emotive imagery technique; doing shame-attacking exercises; doing role-playing and reverse role-playing; making strong disputing audio recordings and regularly listening to them; developing unconditional self-acceptance, unconditional other-acceptance, and unconditional life-acceptance; developing high frustration tolerance;

using reinforcements and penalties; doing appropriate skills training; and applying relapse prevention.

REBT recommends using a good deal of humor. This helps to keep things in perspective and can prevent self-defeating behavior that may occur when people take themselves, others, and life events and conditions too seriously. In the absence of humor and healthy perspective, most humans easily catastrophize and awfulize.

REBT recommends that individuals be diligent and not succumb to the tyranny of the shoulds and musturbation by disputing and rethinking such demandingness. The three major musts to look out for and dispute are the following:

- "I *must* do well and be loved and approved by others."
- "Other people *must* treat me fairly, kindly, and well."
- "The world and my living conditions *must* be comfortable, gratifying, and just, providing me with all that I want in life."

It is recommended in REBT that individuals act with enlightened self-interest. I suggest that an important part of this, in addition to what has already been written, is having and demonstrating discernment about the people we choose to be around us. At times, people have limited choice—for example, they may have family members they can't kick out of their lives or work colleagues and bosses whom they can't get rid of, and they want to keep their jobs despite these difficult others. In such instances, REBT recommends taking the attitude of tolerance and working at developing high frustration tolerance. REBT recommends embracing the challenge of doing so, using coping statements such as, "I can stand what I don't like" and "I can still enjoy life, even when I don't enjoy every person currently in it."

However, when choice is possible, I urge people to be wisely selective about the people in their lives, choosing those who have proven themselves trustworthy, are ethical in their philosophy of life and behavior, have important values similar to their own, and are kind. Having unconditional other-acceptance—which, as you've already read, is one of REBT's emphasized philosophies—does not mean allowing people who act in harmful ways to be around you. By unconditionally accepting them and acknowledging that they are fallible human beings who are acting badly but that they are not 100% bad, you prevent yourself from being enraged and embittered. You may even feel compassion for them. You will then be unlikely to act out self-destructively against them. So you remain sane and emotionally sound. This does not mean, however, that you do not do what you can to stop any improper action from them or that you allow them to stay in your life significantly (or at all).

Discernment, discernment, and more discernment is called for.

REBT recommends that people involve themselves in healthy causes and absorbing interests and activities, with an appreciation for creative expression and pursuit. When one lives in a social group, it is a good thing to have social interest, as Alfred Adler (1929) showed. REBT encourages us to express and demonstrate helping and caring for others and for wider environmental causes around.

REBT reminds us of the benefit and importance of being mindful and of choosing to experience gratitude, wonder, and awe in our daily lives.

Life is brief.

Time moves quickly.

REBT encourages all to accept that despite suffering and challenge in life, there can still be joy when one accepts and applies REBT's principles, practices, and techniques; when individuals are mindful and appreciative of the good and positive things and possibilities in their lives; and when each individual chooses to suffer less misery and to create greater happiness and fulfillment. I hope that REBT will continue to be embraced and practiced by more and more people and that many trained individuals will continue to teach it and use it in their practices. I also hope that it will continue to be validated in research projects.

It is my heartfelt desire that REBT continues to help millions to help themselves; that it becomes more specific and profound, ever relevant to the times; and that it continues to grow, flourish, and thrive. I predict it will.

Because for those who work it—it works!

Glossary of Key Terms

ABC THEORY OF REBT (ABCS)   The formula describing the creation of emotional disturbance. A is the activating event, or *adversity*. B is a *belief* or *belief system* (beliefs may be rational, irrational, or both). C is the *consequence* (which is emotional, behavioral, or both). $A \times B = C$.

AWFULIZE   To believe that a bad, unfortunate, or inconvenient circumstance is more than bad, it is the worst it could be—100% rotten. Doing so is overgeneralizing and exaggerating reality and results in panic, depression, or other debilitating emotions.

CATASTROPHIZE   As in awfulizing, to catastrophize is to inflate and exaggerate reality negatively, to irrationally believe that bad or inconvenient circumstances are utterly catastrophic events. As in awfulizing, catastrophizing results in panic, anxiety, or other unhealthy and disabling emotions.

DISPUTING   The process through which irrational beliefs are forcefully challenged, with the goal of weakening them and ultimately no longer believing them. The three main forms of disputation are realistic disputing, logical disputing, and pragmatic disputing.

EFFECTIVE NEW PHILOSOPHIES   Rational understandings that emerge as a result of disputing irrational beliefs. These include preferences and wishes and avoiding demands. Effective new philosophies are factual and realistic, not exaggerated, and not overgeneralizations. They are goal- and life-enhancing, are flexible, and do not lead to damning oneself, others, or the world.

ELEGANT SOLUTIONS IN PSYCHOTHERAPY   Such solutions seek to change underlying irrational and self-defeating philosophies into rational and life-enhancing ones to effect the profound changes of reduced disturbance and disturbability, changes that can become permanent. In contrast, inelegant solutions deal simply with the outer symptoms of disturbance and attempt solely practical solutions to the presenting issues.

EXPOSURE   One of the REBT behavioral techniques involving the confronting of symptom-provoking situations and the working through of their accompanying thoughts and feelings.

HEALTHY NEGATIVE EMOTIONS   Appropriate, nondebilitating emotional responses to not getting what one wants or to getting what one does not want. These responses result from thinking rationally. Healthy negative emotions include annoyance, frustration, concern, sorrow, regret, sadness, and disappointment.

HIGH FRUSTRATION TOLERANCE (HFT)   The anti-awfulizing philosophy of tolerating and accepting inevitable annoyances in life that one does not prefer, like, or want. It minimizes impatience and prevents rage.

IN VIVO DESENSITIZATION   An REBT behavioral technique that uses a graduated series of assignments in which one does what one is afraid of (harmless actions) to overcome the fear. In vivo desensitization is usually done with gradually increasing degrees of intensity.

IRRATIONAL BELIEFS (IBs)   Self-defeating beliefs that lead to debilitating and unhealthy negative emotions. These include rigid demandingness; awfulizing and catastrophizing; and damning of self, others, and life. They are not founded in facts or reality, they exaggerate or distort truth, and they involve low frustration tolerance.

LOW FRUSTRATION TOLERANCE (LFT)   Opposite of high frustration tolerance, involving whining, moaning, screaming, and not accepting the disappointment of not having what one wants when one wants it. LFT creates unhealthy states, such as discomfort, disturbance, rage, self-pity, and depression.

MULTIMODAL   Using many therapeutic techniques, as REBT does, such as cognitive, emotive, and behavioral techniques.

MUSTURBATION   Rigidly demanding that things *must* be the way one believes they should be; absolutist thinking. Musturbation frequently results in anxiety, depression, and rage.

PYA   Push your ass—a means of making an effort to overcome LFT and to implement REBT procedures. (Also known as PMA, Push my ass.)

RATIONAL BELIEFS   Reality-based beliefs that contribute to the creation of appropriate and healthy emotions. They are nondemanding and include wants and preferences. They encompass unconditional acceptance of self, others, and life; are based on fact; take a healthy; nonexaggerated view; and include high frustration tolerance.

RATIONAL EMOTIVE BEHAVIOR THERAPY (REBT)   The pioneering cognitive behavior therapy, described in this book, humanistic and pragmatic, that revolutionized psychotherapy in the 20th century, influenced major approaches that followed it, and continues to be the most holistic of therapeutic modalities.

SECONDARY SYMPTOMS   Symptoms about one's symptoms, such as panic about one's panic, anxiety about anxiety, and self-downing and then downing oneself for it.

TYRANNY OF THE SHOULDS   Karen Horney's (1950) idealized-image notions with which we afflict ourselves. The tyranny of the shoulds means allowing ourselves to be plagued by the ideas that we should, ought, or must live up to self-invented pictures of the way we should be.

UNCONDITIONAL LIFE-ACCEPTANCE (ULA)   Unconditionally accepting life and the world, including its unfair and rotten aspects. REBT does not condone injustice, unfairness, or rotten acts and encourages doing what one can to right wrongs. However, ULA urges us to do so without resentment and with graceful acceptance of what cannot be changed at the present time.

UNCONDITIONAL OTHER-ACCEPTANCE (UOA)   Unconditionally accepting all others, even when they act in evil ways; disliking others' sins but not overgeneralizing and seeing them as total sinners. UOA urges us to remember that each of us is a fallible and flawed being and to have humility and compassion for human flaws.

UNCONDITIONAL SELF-ACCEPTANCE (USA)   Unconditionally accepting oneself, with one's flaws and failings. USA urges us to learn from our mistakes but not to put ourselves down or falsely think we, in totality, are mistakes or failures. It encourages us to know that our worth as humans exists just because we exist and not as a result of acting in any good, pure, or saintly ways. USA means determinedly accepting and respecting one's self and totality, whether or not one performs well and gains approval of others.

UNHEALTHY NEGATIVE EMOTIONS   Debilitating emotions arising from irrational beliefs. These include serious anxiety, depression, rage, guilt, shame, hurt, jealousy, and low frustration tolerance.

Suggested Readings and Videos

Ellis, A. (2004). *Rational emotive behavior therapy: It works for me, it can work for you.* Amherst, NY: Prometheus Books.

Ellis, A. (2004). *The road to tolerance: The philosophy of rational emotive behavior therapy.* Amherst, NY: Prometheus Books.

Ellis, A. (2005). *The myth of self-esteem.* Amherst, NY: Prometheus Books.

Ellis, A. (2010). *All out: An autobiography.* Amherst, NY: Prometheus Books.

Ellis, A., & Blau, S. (Eds.). (1998). *The Albert Ellis reader.* Secaucus, NJ: Carol.

Ellis, A., & Crawford, T. (2000). *Making intimate connections.* Atascadero, CA: Impact.

Ellis, A., & Ellis, D. J. (2014). *Rational emotive behavior therapy.* In G. R. Vandenbos, E. Meidenbauer, & J. Frank-McNeil (Eds.), *Psychotherapy theories and techniques: A reader* (pp. 289–298). Washington, DC: American Psychological Association.

Ellis, A., & Ellis, D. J. (2014). *Rational emotive behavior therapy process.* In G. R. Vandenbos, E. Meidenbauer, & J. Frank-McNeil (Eds.), *Psychotherapy theories and techniques: A reader* (pp. 299–306). Washington, DC: American Psychological Association.

Ellis, A., & Ellis, D. J. (2019). *Rational emotive behavior therapy.* In D. Wedding & R. J. Corsini (Eds.), *Current psychotherapies* (11th ed.), pp. 157–198. Belmont, CA: Brooks/Cole, Cengage Learning.

Ellis, A., & Harper, R. A. (1961). *A guide to rational living.* Chatsworth, CA: Wilshire Book Company.

Ellis, A., & Harper, R. A. (2003). *Dating, mating, and relating.* New York, NY: Citadel.

Ellis, A., & Knaus, W. (1977). *Overcoming procrastination.* New York, NY: New American Library.

Ellis, D. J. (2014). *Rational emotive behavior therapy* [DVD]. Systems of Psychotherapy video series. Available from https://www.apa.org/pubs/videos/4310919.aspx

Ellis, D. J. (2014). *Counseling and psychotherapy transcripts: REBT with client.* Alexandria, VA: Alexander Street Press.

Ellis, D. J. (2015). *1. On being an effective, empowering and compassionate therapist. 2. Rational emotive behavior therapy: The theory of a comprehensive cognitive behavior therapy. 3. Rational emotive behavior therapy: Tools, techniques and practice* [three-disc DVD set]. Great Teachers, Great Courses series. Alexandria, VA: Alexander Street Press. Available at https://www.academicvideostore.com/series/great-teachers-great-courses

Ellis, D. J. (2015). The profound impact of gratitude: In times of ease and times of challenge. *Spirituality in Clinical Practice, 2*(1), 96–100.

Ellis, D. J. (2015). *Zapping anxiety and depression, and healing trauma, with the vigorous and compassionate approach of rational emotive behavior therapy* [two-disc audio CD set]. Phoenix, AZ: The Milton H. Erickson Foundation.

Ellis, D. J. (2017). Journeying with Meichenbaum: A review of *The evolution of cognitive behavior therapy: A personal and professional journey with Don Meichenbaum. PsycCRITIQUES, 62,* Article 4.

Ellis, D. J. (2017). Rational emotive behavior therapy and individual psychology [Special issue]. *Journal of Individual Psychology, 73,* 272–282.

Ellis, D. J. (2017). Managing stress in a stressful world [Reflection]. In G. Corey, M. Muratori, J. T. Austin II, & J. A. Austin, *Counselor self-care* (pp. 122–123). Alexandria, VA: American Counseling Association.

Ellis, D. J., & Eckstein, D. (2011). Al Ellis: Up close and personal. *The Family Journal: Counseling and Therapy for Couples and Families, 19,* 407–411.

Ellis, D. J., & Ivey, A. (2015, December 23). Getting to know (and love) Albert Ellis and his theory. *Counseling Today.* Retrieved from https://ct.counseling.org/2015/12/getting-to-know-and-love-albert-ellis-and-his-theory/

Ellis, D. J., & Mishlove, J. (2016). *Ellis, Debbie Joffe Interview with Jeffrey Mishlove, Parts One & Two.* New Thinking Allowed video interview series. Available at https://www.youtube.com/watch?v=C7GyIGBxW4k&feature=youtu.be and https://www.youtube.com/watch?v=Vye_SN4XUes&feature=youtu.be

Emmons, R. A., & McCullough, M. E. (2003). Counting blessings versus burdens: An experimental investigation of gratitude and subjective well-being in daily life. *Journal of Personality and Social Psychology, 84,* 377–389.

Epictetus. (1890). *The works of Epictetus.* Boston, MA: Little, Brown.

Halasz, G. (2004). In conversation with Albert Ellis. *Australasian Psychiatry, 12,* 325–333.

Kant, I. (1929). *Critique of pure reason.* New York, NY: St. Martins.

Russell, B. (1965). *The basic writings of Bertrand Russell.* New York, NY: Simon & Schuster.

References

Adler, A. (1929). *The science of living*. New York, NY: Greenberg.

Adler, A. (1931). *What life should mean to you*. New York, NY: Blue Ribbon Books.

Adler, A. (1964). *Social interest: A challenge to mankind*. New York, NY: Capricorn.

Alford, B. A., & Beck, A. T. (1997). *The integrative power of cognitive therapy*. New York, NY: Guilford Press.

American Psychiatric Association. (2007). *Practice guideline for the treatment of patients with OCD*. Arlington, VA: Author.

American Psychiatric Association. (2013). *Diagnostic and statistical manual of mental disorders* (5th ed.). Washington, DC: Author.

American Psychological Association. (2017). *Multicultural guidelines: An ecological approach to context, identity, and intersectionality*. Retrieved from http://www.apa.org/about/policy/multicultural-guidelines.pdf

Bandura, A. (1997). *Self-efficacy: The exercise of control*. New York, NY: Freeman.

Barlow, D. H. (1988). *Anxiety and its disorders: The nature and treatment of anxiety and panic*. New York, NY: Guilford Press.

Barlow, D. H., Esler, J. L., & Vitali, A. E. (1998). Psycho-social treatments for panic disorders, phobias, and generalized anxiety disorder. In P. E. Nathan & J. M. Gorman (Eds.), *A guide to treatments that work* (pp. 288–318). New York, NY: Oxford University Press.

Baucom, D. H., & Epstein, N. (1990). *Cognitive-behavioral marital therapy*. New York, NY: Brunner/Mazel.

Beck, A. T. (1963). Thinking and depression. I. Idiosyncratic content and cognitive distortions. *Archives of General Psychiatry, 9*, 324–333. http://dx.doi.org/10.1001/archpsyc.1963.01720160014002

Beck, A. T. (1976). *Cognitive therapy and the emotional disorders*. New York, NY: International Universities Press.

Beck, A. T. (1988). *Love is not enough.* New York, NY: Harper and Row.

Beck, A. T., Rush, A. J., Shaw, B. F., & Emery, G. (1979). *Cognitive therapy of depression.* New York, NY: Guilford Press.

Beck, J. S. (1995). *Cognitive therapy: Basics and beyond.* New York, NY: Guilford Press.

Benjamin, L. S. (1996). *Interpersonal diagnosis and treatment of personality disorders.* New York, NY: Guilford Press.

Bernheim, H. (1947). *Suggestive therapeutics.* New York, NY: London Book Company.

Blau, S., Fuller, J. R., & Vaccaro, T. P. (2006). Rational-emotive disputing and the five-factor model: Personality dimensions of the Ellis Emotional Efficiency Inventory. *Journal of Rational-Emotive & Cognitive-Behavior Therapy, 24,* 87–100. http://dx.doi.org/10.1007/s10942-005-0020-z

Burns, D. D. (1980). *Feeling good: The new mood therapy.* New York, NY: Morrow.

Butler, A. C., Chapman, J. E., Forman, E. M., & Beck, A. T. (2006). The empirical status of cognitive-behavioral therapy: A review of meta-analyses. *Clinical Psychology Review, 26*(1), 17–31. http://dx.doi.org/10.1016/j.cpr.2005.07.003

Carey, B. (2006, January 1). Judge orders psychologist reinstated to institute. *The New York Times.*

Christopher and Dana Reeve Foundation. (2010). *Christopher Reeve: Biography.* Retrieved from http://www.christopherreeve.org/site/c.ddJFKRNoFiG/b.4431483/

Cloninger, F. (2000). *Personality and psychopathology.* Washington, DC: American Psychiatric Association.

Costa, P. T., Jr., & McCrae, R. R. (1992a). The five-factor model of personality and its relevance to personality disorders. *Journal of Personality Disorders, 6,* 343–359. http://dx.doi.org/10.1521/pedi.1992.6.4.343

Costa, P. T., Jr., & McCrae, R. R. (1992b). Normal personality assessment in clinical practice: The NEO personality inventory. *Psychological Assessment, 4,* 5–13. http://dx.doi.org/10.1037/1040-3590.4.1.5

Coué, É. (1923). *My method.* New York, NY: Doubleday Page.

Dalai Lama & Cutler, H. C. (1998). *The art of happiness: A handbook for living.* New York, NY: Riverhead.

David, D., Cotet, C., Matu, S., Mogoase, C., & Stefan, S. (2018). 50 years of rational-emotive and cognitive-behavioral therapy: A systematic review and meta-analysis. *Journal of Clinical Psychology, 74,* 304–318. http://dx.doi.org/10.1002/jclp.22514

David, D., Szentagotai, A., Lupu, V., & Cosman, D. (2008). Rational emotive behavior therapy, cognitive therapy, and medication in the treatment of major depressive disorder: A randomized clinical trial, posttreatment outcomes, and six-month follow-up. *Journal of Clinical Psychology, 64,* 728–746. http://dx.doi.org/10.1002/jclp.20487

Dryden, W., & David, D. (2008). Rational emotive behavior therapy: Current status. *Journal of Cognitive Psychotherapy, 22*, 195–209. http://dx.doi.org/10.1891/0889-8391.22.3.195

Dubois, P. (1907). *The psychic treatment of nervous disorders.* New York, NY: Funk and Wagnalls.

Dyer, W. (1977). *Your erroneous zones.* New York, NY: Avon Books.

Ellis, A. (1956, August). *Rational psychotherapy.* Paper presented at the American Psychological Association Annual Convention, Chicago, IL.

Ellis, A. (1957a). *How to live with a neurotic: At home and at work.* New York, NY: Crown.

Ellis, A. (1957b). Outcome of employing three techniques of psychotherapy. *Journal of Clinical Psychology, 13*, 344–350. http://dx.doi.org/10.1002/1097-4679(195710)13:4<344::AID-JCLP2270130407>3.0.CO;2-9

Ellis, A. (1958). Rational psychotherapy. *Journal of General Psychology, 59*, 35–49. http://dx.doi.org/10.1080/00221309.1958.9710170

Ellis, A. (1962). *Reason and emotion in psychotherapy.* Secaucus, NJ: Citadel.

Ellis, A. (1976). The biological basis of human irrationality. *Journal of Individual Psychology, 32*, 145–168.

Ellis, A. (1979a). Discomfort anxiety: A new cognitive behavioral construct. Part 1. *Rational Living, 14*(2), 3–8.

Ellis, A. (1979b). Discomfort anxiety: A new cognitive behavioral construct. Part 2. *Rational Living, 15*(1), 25–30.

Ellis, A. (1985). *Overcoming resistance: Rational emotive therapy with difficult clients.* New York, NY: Springer.

Ellis, A. (1993). Changing rational emotive therapy (RET) to rational emotive behavior therapy (REBT). *Behavior Therapist, 16*, 257–258.

Ellis, A. (1994). *Reason and emotion in psychotherapy* (Rev. ed.). New York, NY: Citadel.

Ellis, A. (1998). *How to control your anxiety before it controls you.* New York, NY: Citadel.

Ellis, A. (1999). *How to make yourself happy and remarkably less disturbable.* San Luis Obispo, CA: Impact.

Ellis, A. (2001a). *Feeling better, getting better, staying better.* Atascadero, CA: Impact.

Ellis, A. (2001b). *Overcoming destructive beliefs, feelings, and behaviors.* Amherst, NY: Prometheus Books.

Ellis, A. (2002). *Overcoming resistance: A rational emotive behavior therapy integrative approach.* New York, NY: Springer.

Ellis, A. (2003a). *Anger: How to live with and without it* (Rev. ed.). New York, NY: Citadel Press.

Ellis, A. (2003b). *Sex without guilt in the twenty-first century*. Teaneck, NJ: Battle-side Books.

Ellis, A. (2003c). Similarities and differences between rational emotive behavior therapy and cognitive therapy. *Journal of Cognitive Psychotherapy, 17,* 225–240.

Ellis, A. (2004). *Rational emotive behavior therapy: It works for me, it can work for you.* Amherst, NY: Prometheus Books.

Ellis, A. (2005a). Discussion of Christine A. Padesky and Aaron T. Beck, "Science and Philosophy: Comparison of Cognitive Therapy and Rational Emotive Behavior Therapy." *Journal of Cognitive Psychotherapy, 19,* 181–185.

Ellis, A. (2005b). *The myth of self-esteem.* Amherst, NY: Prometheus Books.

Ellis, A. (2010). *All out!: An autobiography.* Amherst, NY: Prometheus Books.

Ellis, A., & Bernard, M. (Eds.). (2006). *Rational emotive behavioral approaches to childhood disorders: Theory, practice and research.* New York, NY: Springer Science+Business Media.

Ellis, A., & Ellis, D. J. (2011). *Rational emotive behavior therapy.* Washington, DC: American Psychological Association.

Ellis, A., & Ellis, D. J. (2019). *Rational emotive behavior therapy.* In D. Wedding & R. J. Corsini (Eds.), *Current psychotherapies* (11th ed., pp. 157–198). Belmont, CA: Brooks/Cole, Cengage Learning.

Ellis, A., & Harper, R. A. (1961). *A guide to rational living.* Chatsworth, CA: Wilshire Book Company.

Ellis, A., & Harper, R. A. (1975). *A guide to rational living* (2nd ed.). Chatsworth, CA: Wilshire Book Company.

Ellis, A., & Harper, R. A. (1997). *A guide to rational living* (3rd ed.). Chatsworth, CA: Wilshire Book Company.

Ellis, A., & Joffe, D. (2002). A study of volunteer clients who experienced live sessions of rational emotive behavior therapy in front of a public audience. *Journal of Rational-Emotive & Cognitive-Behavior Therapy, 20,* 151–158. http://dx.doi.org/10.1023/A:1019828718532

Ellis, A., & Velten, E. (1992). *When AA doesn't work for you: Rational steps for quitting alcohol.* Fort Lee, NJ: Barricade Books.

Ellis, A., & Whiteley, J. (1979). *Theoretical and empirical foundations of rational-emotive therapy.* Pacific Grove, CA: Brooks/Cole.

Ellis, D. J. (2010). Albert Ellis PhD: Master therapist, pioneer, humanist. *Psychological Hypnosis: APA Bulletin of Division 30, 19,* 7–12.

Ellis, D. J. (2015). The profound impact of gratitude: In times of ease and times of challenge. *Spirituality in Clinical Practice, 2*(1), 96–100. http://dx.doi.org/10.1037/scp0000051

Emmelkamp, P. M., & Beens, H. (1991). Cognitive therapy with obsessive-compulsive disorder: A comparative evaluation. *Behaviour Research and Therapy, 29,* 293–300. http://dx.doi.org/10.1016/0005-7967(91)90120-R

Emmons, R. A., & McCullough, M. E. (2003). Counting blessings versus burdens: An experimental investigation of gratitude and subjective well-being in daily life. *Journal of Personality and Social Psychology, 84*(2), 377–389. http://dx.doi.org/10.1037/0022-3514.84.2.377

Engels, G. I., Garnefski, N., & Diekstra, R. F. W. (1993). Efficacy of rational-emotive therapy: A quantitative analysis. *Journal of Consulting and Clinical Psychology, 61,* 1083–1090. http://dx.doi.org/10.1037/0022-006X.61.6.1083

Faucher, A., & Kiely, P. (1955). Viellecse: Strategies cognitive et processes de devil. In D. L. Bassett (Ed.), *La devil commeprocessus deguerison* (pp. 42–50). Montreal, Ontario, Canada: Publications MNH.

Freud, S. (1965). *Standard edition of the complete psychological works of Sigmund Freud.* New York, NY: Basic Books.

Frew, J., & Spiegler, M. (2012). *Contemporary psychotherapies for a diverse world* (1st rev. ed.). New York, NY: Routledge.

Friedman, M. J. (1994). Posttraumatic stress disorder. In R. J. Corsini (Ed.), *Encyclopedia of psychology: Vol. 3. M–Q* (2nd ed., pp. 102–104). New York, NY: Wiley.

Gaviţa, O. A., David, D., Bujoreanu, S., Tiba, A., & Ionuţiu, D. R. (2012). The efficacy of a short cognitive–behavioral parent program in the treatment of externalizing behavior disorders in Romanian foster care children: Building parental emotion-regulation through unconditional self- and child-acceptance strategies. *Children and Youth Services Review, 34,* 1290–1297. http://dx.doi.org/10.1016/j.childyouth.2012.03.001

Gill, R. E. (2010, July/August). Program hopes to reduce PTSD—Army to train its own in positive psychology. *The National Psychologist, 19,* 6.

Glasser, W. (1965). *Reality therapy.* New York, NY: Harper.

Glasser, W. (1998). *Choice therapy.* San Francisco, CA: HarperCollins.

Haley, J. (1997). Leaving home: The therapy of disturbed young people. New York, NY: Routledge.

Hayes, S. C., Jacobson, M. S., Follette, V. M., & Dougher, M. J. (1994). *Acceptance and change: Content and context in psychotherapy.* Reno, NV: Contact Press.

Hayes, S. C., Strosahl, K., & Wilson, K. G. (1999). *Acceptance and commitment therapy.* New York, NY: Guilford Press.

Heesacker, M., Heppner, P. P., & Rogers, M. E. (1982). Classics and emerging classics in counseling psychology. *Journal of Counseling Psychology, 29,* 400–405. http://dx.doi.org/10.1037/0022-0167.29.4.400

Herzberg, A. (1945). *Active psychotherapy*. New York, NY: Grune & Stratton.

Hollon, S. D., & Beck, A. T. (1994). Cognitive and cognitive-behavioral therapies. In A. E. Bergin & S. L. Garfield (Eds.), *Handbook of psychotherapy and behavior change* (4th ed., pp. 428–466). New York, NY: Wiley.

Horney, K. (1950). *Neurosis and human growth*. New York, NY: Norton.

Ivey, A., Ivey, M. B., & Zalaquett, C. (2018). *Intentional interviewing and counseling: Facilitating client development in a multicultural society* (9th ed.). Belmont, CA: Cengage Learning.

Jacobson, N. S. (1992). Behavioral couple therapy: A new beginning. *Behavior Therapy, 23*, 493–506. http://dx.doi.org/10.1016/S0005-7894(05)80218-7

Janet, P. (1898). *Neuroses of idée fixes*. Paris, France: Alcan.

Johnson, W. B. (2001). To dispute or not to dispute: Ethical REBT with religious clients. *Cognitive and Behavioral Practice, 8*, 39–47. http://dx.doi.org/10.1016/S1077-7229(01)80042-0

Johnson, W. B. (2008). Rational emotive behavior therapy and the God image. In G. Moriarty & L. Hoffman (Eds.), *God image handbook: Research, theory, and practice* (pp. 157–182). New York, NY: Haworth.

Johnson, W. B. (2016a). Challenging clinically salient religion: The art of respectful confrontation. *Spirituality in Clinical Practice, 3*(1), 10–13.

Johnson, W. B. (2016b). Confrontation of clinically salient religion in psychotherapy: Ethical considerations. *Journal of Psychology and Christianity, 35*, 344–356.

Johnson, W. B., Ridley, C. R., & Nielsen, S. (2000). Religiously sensitive rational emotive behavior therapy: Elegant solutions and ethical risks. *Professional Psychology: Research and Practice, 31*(1), 14–20. http://dx.doi.org/10.1037/0735-7028.31.1.14

Joyce, M. R. (1995). Emotional relief for parents: Is rational-emotive parent education effective? *Journal of Rational-Emotive & Cognitive-Behavior Therapy, 13*(1), 55–75. http://dx.doi.org/10.1007/BF02354557

Kelly, G. (1955). *The psychology of personal constructs*. New York, NY: Norton.

Keyes, K., Jr. (1972). *Handbook to higher consciousness*. Berkeley, CA: Living Love Center.

Korzybski, A. (1933). *Science and sanity*. Concord, CA: International Society for General Semantics.

Lambert, M. J. (2013). Outcome in psychotherapy: The past and important advances. *Psychotherapy, 50*, 42–51. http://dx.doi.org/10.1037/a0030682

Lazarus, A. A. (1989). *The practice of multimodal therapy*. Baltimore, MD: The Johns Hopkins University Press.

Lazarus, A. A. (1997). *Brief but comprehensive therapy: The multimodal way*. New York, NY: Springer.

Lazarus, R. S. (1966). *Psychological stress and the coping process*. New York, NY: Springer.

Lazarus, R. S., & Folkman, S. (1984). *Stress, appraisal, and coping*. New York, NY: Springer.

Linehan, M. (1993). *Cognitive behavioral treatment of borderline personality disorder*. New York, NY: Guilford Press.

Lyons, L. C., & Woods, P. J. (1991). The efficacy of rational-emotive therapy: A quantitative review of the outcome research. *Clinical Psychology Review, 11*, 357–369. http://dx.doi.org/10.1016/0272-7358(91)90113-9

Macaskill, N. D., & Macaskill, A. (1996). Rational-emotive therapy plus pharmacotherapy versus pharmacotherapy alone in the treatment of high cognitive dysfunction depression. *Cognitive Therapy and Research, 20*, 575–592. http://dx.doi.org/10.1007/BF02227962

Mahoney, M. J. (1991). *Human change processes*. New York, NY: Basic Books.

Maultsby, M. C., Jr. (1971). Rational emotive imagery. *Rational Living, 6*, 24–27.

Maultsby, M. C., Jr. (1984). *Rational emotive therapy*. Englewood Cliffs, NJ: Prentice-Hall.

McGovern, T. E., & Silverman, M. S. (1984). A review of outcome studies of rational-emotive therapy from 1977 to 1982. *Journal of Rational-Emotive Therapy, 2*(1), 7–18. http://dx.doi.org/10.1007/BF02283004

Meaden, A., Keen, N., Aston, R., Barton, K., & Bucci, S. (2013). *Cognitive therapy for command hallucinations: An advanced practical companion*. New York, NY: Routledge. http://dx.doi.org/10.4324/9780203086544

Meichenbaum, D. (1977). *Cognitive behavior modification*. New York, NY: Plenum. http://dx.doi.org/10.1007/978-1-4757-9739-8

Meichenbaum, D. (1997). The evolution of a cognitive-behavior therapist. In J. K. Zeig (Ed.), *The evolution of psychotherapy: The third conference* (pp. 95–106). New York, NY: Brunner/Mazel.

Mersch, P. P. A., Emmelkamp, P. M., Bögels, S. M., & van der Sleen, J. (1989). Social phobia: Individual response patterns and the effects of behavioral and cognitive interventions. *Behaviour Research and Therapy, 27*, 421–434. http://dx.doi.org/10.1016/0005-7967(89)90013-2

Montgomery, G. H., David, D., Kangas, M., Green, S., Sucala, M., Bovbjerg, D. H., ... Schnur, J. B. (2014). Randomized controlled trial of a cognitive-behavioral therapy plus hypnosis intervention to control fatigue in patients undergoing radiotherapy for breast cancer. *Journal of Clinical Oncology, 32*, 557–563. http://dx.doi.org/10.1200/JCO.2013.49.3437

Nielsen, S., Johnson, W. B., & Ellis, A. (2001). *Counseling and psychotherapy with religious persons: A rational emotive behavior therapy approach*. Mahwah, NJ: Erlbaum. http://dx.doi.org/10.4324/9781410600707

Nielsen, S., Johnson, W. B., & Ridley, C. R. (2000). Religiously sensitive rational emotive behavior therapy: Theory, techniques, and brief excerpts from a case. *Professional Psychology: Research and Practice, 31*(1), 21–28. http://dx.doi.org/10.1037/0735-7028.31.1.21

Norcross, J. C., & Lambert, M. J. (2011). Evidence-based therapy relationships. In J. C. Norcross (Ed.), *Psychotherapy relationships that work: Evidence-based responsiveness* (2nd ed., pp. 3–24). New York, NY: Oxford University Press. http://dx.doi.org/10.1093/acprof:oso/9780199737208.003.0001

Padesky, C. A., & Beck, A. T. (2003). Science and philosophy: Comparison of cognitive therapy and rational emotive behavior therapy. *Journal of Cognitive Psychotherapy, 17*, 211–229.

Paulson, D. S., & Krippner, S. (2007). *Haunted by combat.* Westport, CT: Praeger Security International.

Penn, P. E., & Brooks, A. J. (2000). Five years, twelve steps, and REBT in the treatment of dual diagnosis. *Journal of Rational-Emotive & Cognitive-Behavior Therapy, 18*, 197–208. http://dx.doi.org/10.1023/A:1007883021936

Rigby, K., & Bortolozzo, G. (2013). How schoolchildren's acceptance of self and others relate to their attitudes to victims of bullying. *Social Psychology of Education, 16*(2), 181.

Russell, B. (1950). *The conquest of happiness.* New York, NY: New American Library.

Schnur, J. B., David, D., Kangas, M., Green, S., Bovbjerg, D. H., & Montgomery, G. H. (2009). A randomized trial of a cognitive-behavioral therapy and hypnosis intervention on positive and negative affect during breast cancer radiotherapy. *Journal of Clinical Psychology, 65*, 443–455. http://dx.doi.org/10.1002/jclp.20559

Seligman, M. E. P., & Csikszentmihalyi, M. (2000). Positive psychology [Special issue]. *American Psychologist, 55.* Available from http://psycnet.apa.org/PsycARTICLES/journal/amp/55/1

Seligman, M. E. P., Revich, K., Jaycox, L., & Gillham, J. (1995). *The optimistic child: A proven program to safeguard children against depression and build lifelong resilience.* New York, NY: Houghton-Mifflin.

Shelley, A. M., Battaglia, J., Lucely, J., Ellis, A., & Opler, A. (2001). Symptom-specific group therapy for inpatients with schizophrenia. *The Einstein Quarterly Journal of Biology and Medicine, 18*, 21–28.

Silverman, M. S., McCarthy, M., & McGovern, T. (1992). A review of outcome studies of rational-emotive therapy from 1982–1989. *Journal of Rational-Emotive & Cognitive-Behavior Therapy, 10*, 111–186. http://dx.doi.org/10.1007/BF01061071

Skinner, B. F. (1971). *Beyond freedom and dignity*. New York, NY: Knopf.

Smith, D. (1982). Trends in counseling and psychotherapy. *American Psychologist, 37*, 802–809. http://dx.doi.org/10.1037/0003-066X.37.7.802

Sogyal Rinpoche. (1993). *The Tibetan book of living and dying*. New York, NY: Harper Collins.

VandenBos, G. R. (Ed.). (2015). *APA dictionary of psychology* (2nd ed.). Washington, DC: American Psychological Association.

Velten, E., & Penn, P. E. (2010). *REBT for people with co-occurring problems*. Sarasota, FL: Professional Resource Press.

Wang, C., Jia, F., Fang, R., Zhu, Y., & Huang, Y. (1999). Comparative study of rational-emotive therapy for 95 patients with dysthymic disorder. *Chinese Mental Health Journal, 13*, 172–173.

Warner, R. E. (1991). A survey of theoretical orientations of Canadian clinical psychologists. *Canadian Psychology, 32*, 525–528. http://dx.doi.org/10.1037/h0079025

Watson, J. B. (1919). *Psychology from the standpoint of a behaviorist*. Philadelphia, PA: Lippincott. http://dx.doi.org/10.1037/10016-000

Wedding, D., & Corsini, R. J. (2019). *Current psychotherapies* (11th ed.). Boston, MA: Cengage Learning.

White, M., & Epston, D. (1990). *Narrative means to therapeutic ends*. New York, NY: Norton.

Wolpe, J. (1990). *The practice of behavior therapy* (4th ed.). Needham Heights, MA: Allyn & Bacon.

Woods, P. J. (1992). A study of "belief" and "non-belief" items from the Jones Irrational Beliefs Test with implications for the theory of RET. *Journal of Rational-Emotive & Cognitive-Behavior Therapy, 10*, 41–52. http://dx.doi.org/10.1007/BF01245741

Yager, J. (2015). Updating empathy. *Psychiatry, 78*(2), 134–140.

Index

ABC theory, 27–30, 141
    defined, 145
    in group therapy, 68
    and multimodal nature of REBT, 31
    in OCD case example, 118–119
Abilify, 56
Absolutistic thinking, 28, 44–47, 69–70
    brief therapy to overcome, 55
    in depressive disorders, 87–88
    and Korzybski's theories, 39
    lack of research on, 128
    using rational coping philosophies to overcome, 47
Acceptance and commitment therapy, 139
Action, focus on, 12
Activating events (in ABC theory), 27–28, 145
Active-directive therapy, 11–12, 86
Addictions (addictiveness), 100–103, 135
Adler, Alfred, 15, 30, 127, 128, 143
Adversity (in ABC theory), 22, 28, 101, 145
Albert Ellis Institute, 125
All Out! (Ellis), 9, 18

American Psychological Association (APA), 13
American Psychologist, 128
Anafranil (clomipramine), 117
Anger, extreme, 95–97
Antidepressants, 87, 92
Anti-musturbation, 46–47
Anxietizing, 71, 99
Anxiety disorders, 71–86
APA (American Psychological Association), 13
Approval, need for, 71, 73
Awfulizing, 69
    defined, 145
    in depressive disorders, 88–91
    in posttraumatic stress disorder, 108
    use of rational coping philosophies to overcome, 48

Backsliding, 68, 69
Bandura, Albert, 31, 111
Barlow, David, 30
Baucam, D. H., 127–128
Beck, Aaron T., 6
    on cognitive behavior therapy, 30, 35, 126, 134
    on cognitive therapy, 14–15, 139
    on family relationship therapy, 128

About the Authors

Albert Ellis, PhD, was born in Pittsburgh on September 27, 1913, and raised in New York City. He received his MA and PhD degrees in clinical psychology from Columbia University in New York City. Dr. Ellis held many important psychological positions, including chief psychologist of the state of New Jersey and adjunct professorships at Rutgers and other universities. He practiced psychotherapy, marriage and family counseling, and sex therapy for more than 65 years. He was the founder of rational emotive behavior therapy, the first of the cognitive behavior therapies. In 1959, he founded the Albert Ellis Institute, and he was dedicated to its work and growth.

Dr. Ellis served as president of the Division of Consulting Psychology of the American Psychological Association (APA) and of the Society for the Scientific Study of Sexuality. He also served as officer of several professional societies, including the American Association of Marital and Family Therapy; the American Academy of Psychotherapists; and the American Association of Sexuality Educators, Counselors and Therapists. He was a diplomate in clinical psychology for the American Board of Professional Psychology and several other professional boards.

Professional societies that have given Dr. Ellis their highest professional and clinical awards include the APA, the Association for the Advancement of Behavior Therapy, the American Counseling Association, and the American Psychopathological Association. He was ranked as one of the Most

Influential Psychologists by both American and Canadian psychologists and counselors. He served as consulting or associate editor of many scientific journals and published more than 85 books and monographs, including a number of best-selling popular and professional volumes. Some of his best-known books include *How to Live With a "Neurotic" at Home and at Work*; *The Art and Science of Love*; *A Guide to Rational Living*; *Reason and Emotion in Psychotherapy*; *How to Stubbornly Refuse to Make Yourself Miserable About Anything (Yes, Anything!)*; *Overcoming Procrastination*; *Overcoming Resistance*; *The Practice of Rational Emotive Behavior Therapy*; *How to Make Yourself Happy and Remarkably Less Disturbable*; *Feeling Better, Getting Better, Staying Better*; *Overcoming Destructive Beliefs, Feelings, and Behaviors*; *Anger: How to Live With and Without It*; *Ask Albert Ellis*; *Sex Without Guilt in the 21st Century*; *Making Intimate Connections*; *Rational Emotive Behavior Therapy: It Works for Me, It Can Work for You*; *The Road to Tolerance*; and *The Myth of Self-Esteem*. His autobiography, *All Out!*, was released in 2010, to be followed by other books he wrote and coauthored with his wife, Dr. Debbie Joffe Ellis.

Albert Ellis died on July 24, 2007.

Debbie Joffe Ellis, PhD, born and raised in Melbourne, Australia, is a licensed psychologist (Australia) and a licensed mental health counselor (New York). She is an adjunct professor at Columbia University Teachers College in New York City in the Department of Clinical and Counseling Psychology. She is affiliated with several major psychological associations, including the American Psychological Association, the American Group Therapy Association, and the Australian Psychological Society.

She has a doctorate in alternative medicine from the Indian Board of Alternative Medicines in affiliation with the World Health Organization, from which she has also received a gold medal (1993) in recognition of her service to the field of alternative medicine.

In Australia, Dr. Joffe Ellis worked in her busy private practice; taught college courses on rational emotive behavior therapy, counseling, and personal development; and gave public and professional workshops and presentations. In the United States, she worked with her husband, Albert Ellis, giving public presentations and professional trainings on rational emotive behavior therapy and collaborating on writing and research projects until his death in 2007.

Dedicated to her husband, she continues to present, practice, and write about his brilliant, groundbreaking approach. She currently has a private practice in New York City, and she delivers lectures, workshops, and seminars throughout the United States and across the globe. Visit her website for more information (http://www.debbiejoffeellis.com).

About the Series Editor

Matt Englar-Carlson, PhD, is a professor of counseling and the director of the Center for Boys and Men at California State University–Fullerton. As a scholar, teacher, and clinician, Dr. Englar-Carlson focuses on training clinicians to work more effectively with their male clients across the full range of human diversity. He has over 50 publications and 75 national and international presentations, most of which are focused on men and masculinity, social justice and diversity issues in psychological training and practice, and theories of psychotherapy. Dr. Englar-Carlson coedited the books *In the Room With Men: A Casebook of Therapeutic Change, Counseling Troubled Boys: A Guidebook for Professionals, Beyond the 50-Minute Hour: Therapists Involved in Meaningful Social Action,* and *A Counselor's Guide to Working With Men,* and was featured in the APA-produced DVD *Engaging Men in Psychotherapy.* He is an APA fellow, and received the 2007 Researcher of the Year Award and the 2001 Student of the Year Award from APA Division 51, Society for the Psychological Study of Men and Masculinities. As a clinician, Dr. Englar-Carlson has worked with children, adults, and families in school, community, and university mental health settings. He coauthored (with Jon Carlson) *Adlerian Psychotherapy,* which is part of the Theories of Psychotherapy Series.